Language Teaching:
A Scheme for Teacher Education

Editors: C N Candlin and H G Widdow

Listening

Anne Anderson and Tony Lynch

Oxford University Press

Oxford University Press,
Great Clarendon Street, Oxford OX2 6DP

Oxford New York
Auckland Bangkok Buenos Aires Cape Town Chennai Dar es Salaam Delhi
Hong Kong Istanbul Karachi Kolkata Kuala Lumpur Madrid Melbourne
Mexico City Mumbai Nairobi São Paulo Shanghai Taipei Tokyo Toronto

Oxford and *Oxford English* are trade marks of Oxford University Press

ISBN 0 19 437135 2

© Oxford University Press 1988

First published 1988
Eleventh impression 2003

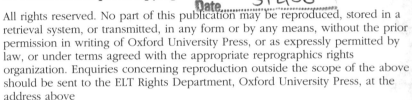

Printed in China

Acknowledgements

The publisher would like to thank the following for their permission to
reproduce material that falls within their copyright:

Cambridge University Press for extracts from *Study Listening* (1983) by
T. Lynch, and *Elementary Task Listening* (1984) by J. S. Stokes.

William Collins, Sons and Co. Ltd. for extracts from *A Listening
Comprehension and Note-taking Course* (1979) by K. James, R. R. Jordan,
and A. Matthews, and *Figures in Language: Describe and Draw* (1982) by
R. R. Jordan.

Longman Group for extracts from *Viewpoints* (1974) by R. O'Neill and
R. Scott, and *Start Listening* (1981) by A. McLean.

Unwin Hyman Ltd. for an extract from *Listening and Note-taking* (1977)
by N. Ferguson and M. O'Reilly.

Scott Windeatt for an extract from 'A project in self-access learning for
English language and study skills' (1980) in *Practical Papers in English
Language Education*, Volume 4 (University of Lancaster).

The publisher would also like to thank the following Oxford University
Press authors for agreeing to the reproduction of extracts from their books:

Mary Underwood for extracts from *Listen to This!* (1971); *What a Story!*
(1976), and *Have You Heard?* (1979).

Mary Underwood and Pauline Barr for extracts from *Listeners*: (Series B:
Work—'Professions' and 'Unsocial Hours')

Contents

Section Two: Demonstration—Listening materials

Section Three: Exploration

The authors and series editors

Anne Anderson studied Psychology at the University of Glasgow where she later obtained a Ph.D. for her research on text comprehension in adult native speakers. Subsequently, she was involved in research projects at the University of Edinburgh, but has now returned to the University of Glasgow where she holds a lectureship in Psychology.

Tony Lynch graduated from Cambridge University in 1971 in Modern Languages and Linguistics. Since 1980 he has worked in English for Academic Purposes and teacher education in the Institute for Applied Language Studies at the University of Edinburgh, where in 1988 he completed a PhD on the grading of listening materials. His main professional interests are (non-)comprehension, materials development, and academic writing skills. He is the author of *Communication in the Language Classroom* (1996).

Christopher N. Candlin is Chair Professor of Applied Linguistics at the City University of Hong Kong. He was formerly Professor of Linguistics in the School of English, Linguistics, and Media, and Executive Director of the National Centre for English Language Teaching and Research at Macquarie University, Sydney, having previously been Professor of Applied Linguistics and Director of the Centre for Language in Social Life at the University of Lancaster. He also co-founded and directed the Institute for English Language Education at Lancaster, where he worked on issues in in-service education for teachers.

Henry Widdowson is Professor of English Linguistics at the University of Vienna, and was previously Professor of English for Speakers of Other Languages at the University of London Institute of Education, and Professor of Applied Linguistics at the University of Essex. Before that he was Lecturer in Applied Linguistics at the University of Edinburgh, and has also worked as an English Language Officer for the British Council in Sri Lanka and Bangladesh.

Through work with The British Council, The Council of Europe, and other agencies, both Editors have had extensive and varied experience of language teaching, teacher education, and curriculum development overseas, and both contribute to seminars, conferences, and professional journals.

Introduction

Listening

There is no shortage of listening materials intended to meet the language teacher's need for interesting and attractive activities. The purpose of this book is to stand back from the surface detail of comprehension materials and to provide an overall perspective on listening as a communicative activity and as a language learning activity.

In Section One we discuss the findings of research into what language comprehension involves, how it relates to the other skills of communication, and to what extent it seems possible to develop comprehension skills both in the mother tongue (L1) and in a foreign language (L2). In particular we look at the notion of grading, which we believe to be the key to the construction of systematic programmes to teach listening.

Section Two deals with issues of immediate concern to the language teacher: On what basis can I choose (or design) listening materials? How can I judge the effectiveness of materials as I use them with my students? We examine the views of listening that underlie commercial materials and illustrate our recent work in the area of comprehension task design, including the results of piloting identical materials with L1 and L2 learners.

The purpose of Section Three is to encourage readers to think about and experiment with the creation of materials appropriate to the needs of their own students, by working on a series of small-scale design and research tasks. The tasks are intended to lead to principled decisions about how best to approach the teaching of listening in the light of the three broad issues dealt with in the first two sections: How much of what is known can I apply? How much of what has been done is likely to be effective? How can I assess my students' improvement as listeners?

We would like to acknowledge the contributions of a number of people who have participated directly or indirectly in the development of this book. In particular, we should mention Professor Gillian Brown of the University of Essex, who directed the 'Listening Comprehension Project' that we worked on during the period 1982–5 at the University of Edinburgh. The project (JHH/190/1) was funded by the Scottish Education Department and we are grateful for this financial support; however, the views expressed in this book are our own and do not necessarily reflect those of the Department.

Our thanks also go to the teachers in Lothian Region secondary schools and staff at the Institute for Applied Language Studies, Edinburgh, who piloted our experimental teaching materials with their L1 and L2 students respectively and agreed to record their classes' performances. The final shape of the book owes much to the influence of the series editors, Henry Widdowson and Chris Candlin. The fact that they moved several thousand miles apart during the writing of the book is coincidental.

Finally, we should draw attention to a stylistic detail, but a non-trivial one. At points in the book we refer to the individual teacher as 'she' and to the individual learner as 'he'. Although this probably reflects the sexual balance of the classroom worldwide, the two pronouns should be read as unmarked forms.

Anne Anderson
Tony Lynch

Language Teaching:
A Scheme for Teacher Education

The purpose of this scheme of books is to engage language teachers in a process of continual professional development. We have designed it so as to guide teachers towards the critical appraisal of ideas and the informed application of these ideas in their own classrooms. The scheme provides the means for teachers to take the initiative themselves in pedagogic planning. The emphasis is on critical enquiry as a basis for effective action.

We believe that advances in language teaching stem from the independent efforts of teachers in their own classrooms. This independence is not brought about by imposing fixed ideas and promoting fashionable formulas. It can only occur where teachers, individually or collectively, explore principles and experiment with techniques. Our purpose is to offer guidance on how this might be achieved.

The scheme consists of three sub-series of books covering areas of enquiry and practice of immediate relevance to language teaching and learning. Sub-series 1 focuses on areas of *language knowledge*, with books linked to the conventional levels of linguistic description: pronunciation, vocabulary, grammar, and discourse. Sub-series 2 (of which this present volume forms a part) focuses on different *modes of behaviour* which realize this knowledge. It is concerned with the pedagogic skills of speaking, listening, reading, and writing. Sub-series 3 focuses on a variety of *modes of action* which are needed if this knowledge and behaviour is to be acquired in the operation of language teaching. The books in this sub-series have do with such topics as syllabus design, the content of language courses, and aspects of methodology and evaluation.

This sub-division of the field is not meant to suggest that different topics can be dealt with in isolation. On the contrary, the concept of a scheme implies making coherent links between all these different areas of enquiry and activity. We wish to emphasize how their integration formalizes the complex factors present in any teaching process. Each book, then, highlights a particular topic, but also deals contingently with other issues, themselves treated as focal in other books in the series. Clearly, an enquiry into a mode of behaviour like speaking, for example, must also refer to aspects of language knowledge which it realizes. It must also connect to modes of action which can be directed at developing this behaviour in learners. As elements of the whole scheme, therefore, books cross-refer both within and across the different sub-series.

This principle of cross-reference which links the elements of the scheme is also applied to the internal design of the different inter-related books within it. Thus, each book contains three sections, which, by a combination of text and task, engage the reader in a principled enquiry into ideas and practices. The first section of each book makes explicit those theoretical ideas which bear on the topic in question. It provides a conceptual framework for those sections which follow. Here the text has a mainly *explanatory* function, and the tasks serve to clarify and consolidate the points raised. The second section shifts the focus of attention to how the ideas from Section One relate to activities in the classroom. Here the text is concerned with *demonstration*, and the tasks are designed to get readers to evaluate suggestions for teaching in reference both to the ideas from Section One and also to their own teaching experience. In the third section this experience is projected into future work. Here the set of tasks, modelled on those in Section Two, are designed to be carried out by the reader as a combination of teaching techniques and action research in the actual classroom. It is this section that renews the reader's contact with reality: the ideas expounded in Section One and linked to pedagogic practice in Section Two are now to be systematically *tested out* in the process of classroom teaching.

If language teaching is to be a genuinely professional enterprise, it requires continual experimentation and evaluation on the part of practitioners whereby in seeking to be more effective in their pedagogy they provide at the same time—and as a corollary—for their own continuing education. It is our aim in this scheme to promote this dual purpose.

Christopher N. Candlin
Henry Widdowson

Explanation
Research into listening

1   What is listening comprehension?

1.1 Introduction

We tend to take listening for granted. Imagine, for example, that you are about to board a bus in a noisy city street. You continue talking to a friend and listening to her replies; you understand when the driver, whose voice you have never heard before, tells you what the fare is; you notice that a small child on the bus has started crying; you realize that the music that had been blaring out of the clothes shop by the bus stop has been switched off. All this happens—or, more exactly, you *accomplish* all this—at the same time and without any noticeable difficulty.

We only become aware of what remarkable feats of listening we achieve when we are in an unfamiliar listening environment, such as listening to a language in which we have limited proficiency. Even managing to separate speech from non-speech sounds seems a real achievement: the other parts of the process which we take for granted in our L1—dividing an unfamiliar speaker's utterances into words, identifying them, and at the same time interpreting what the speaker meant and then preparing an appropriate reply—now become formidable tasks. It is hardly surprising that people everywhere believe that 'foreigners speak too fast'.

Another common problem that we face as L2 learners is that, even if we have carefully rehearsed a particular utterance and manage to produce it to a native speaker, it may well result in a torrent of language from the other person. Our carefully practised request for bread leads to an unintelligible stream (or so it seems) of comment from the shop assistant about the type, quantity, price, or unavailability.

▶ ## TASK 1

We can try to overcome limited proficiency in *speaking* a foreign language by rehearsing what we intend to say. Are there any *listening* situations where rehearsal would be effective? What would be the difference between such situations and ones where rehearsal would be pointless?

This sort of difficulty highlights two facts about listening. Firstly, it shows that listening skills are as important as speaking skills; we cannot communicate face-to-face unless the two types of skill are developed in tandem. Rehearsed production is useless if we are unable to respond to the reply that it generates from our interlocutor (i.e. the person we are trying to talk to).

The second point about listening is that, under many circumstances, it is a reciprocal skill. We cannot practise listening in the same way as we can rehearse speaking, or at least the part of speaking that has to do with pronunciation, because we cannot usually predict what we will have to listen to. In this book we shall be concerned primarily with this kind of reciprocal listening—listening where there is at least the opportunity for speaker and listener to exchange roles—as opposed to the non-reciprocal or one-way listening involved in, for example, listening to the radio.

Listening effectively involves a multiplicity of skills. Let us construct a very simple step-by-step picture of the various elements that might be thought to make up the process of listening in face-to-face conversation:

1 The spoken signals have to be identified from the midst of surrounding sounds.
2 The continuous stream of speech has to be segmented into units, which have to be recognized as known words.
3 The syntax of the utterance has to be grasped and the speaker's intended meaning has to be understood.
4 We also have to apply our linguistic knowledge to formulating a correct and appropriate response to what has been said.

As we shall see (in **2.2**), there is evidence that these listening skills are deployed not as separate steps but *simultaneously*—which makes listening an even more formidable achievement.

This picture of the linguistic side of comprehension is already rather complex, but this is by no means all that is involved in listening. We listen for a *purpose*, not merely as a way of exercising language skills. Since we have non-linguistic purposes in listening, it follows that listening effectively also involves non-linguistic skills.

▶ TASK 2

What are the 'extra' skills needed in listening to the following people?

1 a recently widowed neighbour talking about her husband's funeral
2 a five-year-old describing her birthday party
3 an elderly relative who has become very upset and breathless, trying to tell you where his medicine is kept
4 an official explaining how to make an insurance claim.

Our listening purposes may be primarily social, as in the case of chatting to a stranger to pass the time waiting for a train. Here, the additional skills necessary to the social purpose will include, for example, judging whether the speaker is upset or angry and then making the appropriate sympathetic noises, whether or not we actually understand the reasons for their mood.

Alternatively, our purpose may be primarily to extract information. We might ask the way to a particular destination and have to understand the directions we are then given. In this case, we need to deploy cognitive skills in order to relate the spoken information to the non-linguistic environment in order to decide, for example, how the utterance 'go past the church' relates to our current physical location.

▶ TASK 3

Imagine you are staying in a hotel in a city you do not know well. You have a meeting at an office which you were told is about five minutes' walk away. You need to ask directions to the office. Would it be an easier listening task to get the information by (1) ringing the hotel reception desk, or (2) asking a passer-by outside the hotel? Why?

In discussing the broad distinction between purposes of communication, Brown and Yule (1983a) coined the terms 'interactional talk' and 'transactional talk'. 'Interactional' is used to refer to speech that is primarily social: in 'transactional' communication the main purpose is to achieve a successful transfer or exchange of information. However, the two terms represent what is in fact a continuum, from the social to the informative aspects of listening. Many situations fall in between the two extremes and will therefore require a combination of linguistic and non-linguistic skills. In this book we will examine the kinds of skill that are involved in effective listening, how they develop in native listeners, and what we might do as teachers to facilitate this development in native and non-native listeners.

1.2 What is successful listening?

There are a number of different ways in which the listener can process—or fail to process—incoming speech, which could serve as a basis for evaluating the degree of success of a particular listening performance.

First, the listener *may not hear adequately* what has been said, due, for example, to competing background noise or unfamiliarity with the speaker's accent. Under these circumstances, the speech may have been 'heard' in a strictly limited sense: the listener recognizes that he has been spoken to, but has no idea what the message contained in the speech was.

Second—and this is presumably a common problem for the foreign listener—speech may contain words or phrases that the listener *can hear adequately but is unable to understand* because of serious problems with the syntax or semantics of the foreign language.

Third, there are times when the listener is perfectly able to hear and understand the speaker, but *may have 'switched off'* consciously or unconsciously. For instance we might suddenly remember that we have only ten minutes before the banks close. In this sort of situation it is common to find ourselves allowing the incoming speech from our interlocutor to flow past us as a stream of sound which we make no attempt to process.

Fourth, there are those messages which the listener *attends to fully and from which he tries to construct a coherent interpretation.* We might consider this last situation to be one of maximally co-operative listening, in the sense that the listener is both able and willing to play his part in the reciprocal activity of communication.

Traditionally, listening has often been regarded, alongside reading, as a passive language skill. We have already suggested how it involves *more than language*; we also need to challenge the view that listening is merely 'passive' or 'receptive'. As we hope to show in this book, the role of the successful listener has to be thought of as an *active* one. Understanding is not something that happens because of what a speaker says: the listener has a crucial part to play in the process, by activating various types of knowledge, and by applying what he knows to what he hears and trying to understand what the speaker means.

▶ TASK 4

English makes a distinction between the activities of 'hearing' and 'listening'. What is it? Is the same distinction made in other languages that you know?

We have already suggested that effective listening involves a large number of component skills. Effective listeners actively engage in the process of comprehension: they apply the relevant internal information available to them in order to construct their own interpretation of what has been said. They do not passively receive and record.

▶ TASK 5

Think about the use of the word 'listen' in these four situations. What are the differences between the processes involved in each case?

1 The parents asked the baby-sitter to listen at the child's door every fifteen minutes or so.

2 I had to listen to his complaints about the cost of living for the best part of an hour.

3 The President's spokesman has admitted that a listening device had been placed in the Secretary of State's office.

4 The most important skill a doctor has to learn is to be a good listener.

The teacher or researcher interested in developing or studying listening faces a fundamental problem: it is impossible to gain direct access to the listening process itself. We can never actually observe the problems the student may experience and the skills he uses. Did he pay attention? Was he unfamiliar with the form of the message? Or with the content? Did he try actively to construct an interpretation of what was said? We are able only to deduce what the listeners did with the message and what they found difficult by examining their response—whether spoken, written, or non-verbal.

To try to overcome this basic difficulty, we can set learners tasks that require them to demonstrate in an observable way their comprehension of some aspect of what has been said. However, it is not always easy to pinpoint the stage in the listening process that may have resulted in a less than satisfactory response. We can think of the three parts of the sequence: *input* (the words uttered by the speaker); the *listening process* (the listener's application of various types of information available to him), and *output* (the response from the listener).

We can never be certain that a student actually heard the input adequately, except by trying to ensure that the listening environment is reasonably free from extraneous noise and that the sound level of the input seems satisfactory. Of course, we have to strike a balance between, on the one hand, maximizing the student's chances of performing adequately by providing an ideal listening environment and, on the other, providing practice and experience in a realistic context.

Another aspect of this trade-off between idealized training conditions and the need for realistic preparation for listening outside the classroom is the nature of the tasks we set learners and the responses we require of them. For native listeners, the commonest setting for listener responses is spontaneous conversation. So for L2 learners, too, practice in conversational skills should be an essential part of a language course.

But as Brown and Yule (1983a) point out, friendly casual conversations among native speakers are relatively undemanding on the listener. They are primarily social events. The interlocutors often produce short stock replies which keep the interaction going and add to the general feeling of friendliness, but are relatively informationless. This is because the maintaining of a friendly atmosphere, rather than the exchange of information, is the main reason for this kind of conversation.

It is important that both L1 and L2 learners get sufficient training in the more demanding and equally necessary skills of transactional listening, where the focus of communication is on the exchange of information. These skills are unlikely to be adequately developed through social conversational practice alone. From observing a pair of students engaged in interactional talk we would not be in a position to decide whether the occasional 'uhuh' and 'hmhm' produced by one of them was in fact evidence of full comprehension, partial comprehension, or simply the 'automatic pilot' response of someone who has, as we said earlier, switched off due to boredom, worry, or perhaps the availability of a more interesting topic in another conversation nearby.

▶ TASK 6

In this invented dialogue, **A** is describing how to make a good curry. Pay particular attention to **B**'s responses.

1 Decide whether he is trying to follow and remember what **A** is telling him, or whether he is simply making polite conversational noises.

A: Now the important thing about making curry is the spices. They must be fresh, not out of those horrible little tins you've had at the back of the cupboard for ages.

B: Uhuh.

A: Then you must fry the spices in oil, before you add the meat.

B: In oil, oh.

A: Yes. Then you brown the meat in the spices before you add any liquid.

B: I must remember that. Have you tried that Indian in Elderslie Street? It's really good.

2 What other information would you need in order to be more certain in your judgement of **B**?

All types of listening skill are valuable and necessary if a learner is to acquire an all-round ability to listen effectively in a range of situations, to various types of input, and for a variety of listening purposes. There are two principal reasons for our stressing the importance of listening that is primarily transactional in this book. First, for many students it seems to be the most demanding and is therefore a skill that needs a considerable amount of practice and training. Many native speakers have difficulty with this kind of listening, as we shall see in 2.3 and 7. Second, it is an area of listening which is in danger of being overlooked in courses for foreign learners that focus their listening training on the sound system or grammar of the language, or alternatively on oral practice in friendly, social conversations.

1.3 One view of listening: the listener as tape recorder

We have considered some of the skills required to listen successfully and the problems of trying to assess if the listener has deployed them on a particular occasion. The problem that now arises is how to decide what kind of behaviour is the best test of comprehension. This decision involves more than simply considerations about assessment; it depends on our whole conception of the nature of listening.

We might suppose that one obvious test of the listener's comprehension is his ability to remember the message he has received. If he can reproduce what was said to him, then surely we can say both that he heard the message and that he was paying attention to it—two of the criteria for effective listening that we mentioned in **1.2**. But does this mean we can be sure that the listener has understood what was said? How is listening comprehension related to our ability to remember a spoken message?

▶ TASK 7

Remembers but doesn't understand

1 Your six-year-old niece is very good at remembering poems. Does she 'understand' poetry?

Understands directions but doesn't remember/memorise them.

2 You drive a friend home and she gives you directions on the way. The route is complicated and you have forgotten the details, even immediately after you reach her house. Does this mean you did not understand the directions?

If we were to take the ability to remember a message as the 'acid test' of comprehension, we would in some ways be adopting a view of listening in which the listener acts as a tape recorder. This analogy suggests that, as long as the input is sufficiently loud to be recorded and does not exceed the length of the available blank tape, then the message will be recorded and stored, and can be replayed later.

It might explain some of the differences in the way listeners behave and in the way that different messages are dealt with. For example, we could explain a failure to understand long messages by saying that our mental recorder did not have enough blank tape available to make the recording.

Under some less than ideal listening conditions, our mental recorders might not be able to make a clear recording and so the message might get lost or distorted. If too long a period elapses between recording and replay, we might suppose that our tape deteriorates and, again, the recorded message gets degraded.

We could even conceptualize differences between individual listeners in terms of the tape-recorder analogy. For instance, the L2 listener could be thought of as having the equivalent of a sub-standard cassette recorder which can function only in ideal listening/recording conditions; even then the recording will often be distorted in replay. The adult native listener, on the other hand, might have the equivalent of a top-quality reel-to-reel machine that records sensitively and also replays messages with high fidelity.

▶ TASK 8

Which of the following listening phenomena would (or would not) be explained by the tape-recorder analogy?

1 Some singers learn to give native-like performances of songs in languages they do not know.
2 A university student might recall a lecture in these terms: 'There was a lot of boring stuff about syntax that I didn't get, but she was quite interesting on how young kids form two-word utterances.'
3 A foreign student of English reports a World Service news bulletin to a friend who missed it: 'The only bit I got was something about little danger from nuclear fall-out in Britain—at least I think they said little danger.'

The problem with the tape-recorder analogy is that it does not capture all the relevant features of *comprehension*. On occasions both young and foreign listeners can remember input that they do not understand; even adult native listeners do this, although their non-comprehension may be less apparent.

More frequently, though, the opposite is true: listeners can understand far more than they can recall. For many types of listening, it would be inappropriate for us to attempt to remember everything. No native listeners would feel they had listened inadequately to a casual conversation if they failed to remember what had been said to them when they were asked to recall it some time later.

The same is true for transactional listening: if a listener who is unfamiliar with British electrical wiring is being instructed on how to wire a plug, a successfully wired plug is a more direct demonstration of his listening comprehension than is his ability to remember exactly what was said.

The important difference between being able to *use* the information you have heard and the ability to reproduce the message in word-perfect form is that, in order to use the message, you normally have to interpret what was said and relate the speech to the current non-linguistic environment. It is true that there are some listening circumstances which require recall, but this usually involves the kind of active interpretation described in **1.2**, rather than verbatim (or word-for-word) memory. Indeed, the ability to remember something word-for-word does not necessarily involve any such active processing of the input: we may not know whether a listener who is asked to complete a memory task is actually demonstrating any greater skill than a trained parrot.

▶ TASK 9

Can you think of a context in which the listener's ability to remember a spoken message word-perfectly is the best guide to his listening skills?

Can you think of three situations in which the listener's recall is less important than his ability to use the information he has been told?

Unlike a tape recorder or trained parrot, listeners tend to be selective, in terms of what they find most interesting or important or comprehensible in any particular message. This selective response may of course be quite different from what the speaker intended. The way that when listening we *select*, *interpret*, and *summarize* input cannot be incorporated within the tape-recorder analogy.

Any assessment of an unobservable process such as listening is problematic and in Section Two we consider a range of ways of allowing listeners to demonstrate their abilities without relying on memory exercises or even on spoken or written production skills. At this stage, we are less concerned with the details of assessment procedures than with making clear a general point about the tape-recorder view of listening (i.e. equating the ability to remember spoken input with the ability to comprehend it). This, in our view, represents an inappropriate and inadequate view of the listening process.

1.4 An alternative view of listening: the listener as active model builder

In **1.2** we said that in order to listen successfully we have to construct our own 'coherent interpretation' of any spoken message. Both parts of this term are important. First, it needs to be *coherent* both with what we believe has just been said and with what we already know about the speaker, the context, and the world in general. Second, it is an *interpretation*, in the sense that it is our version of what the speaker meant, as far as we are able to assess that meaning.

In discussing this alternative view of what listening involves, we have chosen to use the term 'mental model' (Johnson-Laird 1980) to refer to the listener's 'coherent interpretation'. This emphasizes the constructive (i.e. active) and personal nature of successful listening. The mental model that we build as a representation of a spoken message is the result of our combining the new information in what we have just heard with our previous knowledge and experience.

The role of this previous knowledge—sometimes called 'background knowledge' or 'knowledge of the world'—is central to the way we understand language, whether through listening or reading. The term covers a range of types of knowledge, any of which we may need to draw on in order to reach an adequate comprehension of what someone has said or written. The extent to which we may need to exploit existing information inside our heads, when attempting to understand what someone tells us, should become clear if we consider a real-life example. One of the authors was passing an elderly female stranger in a street in the West End of Glasgow, when she smiled at him and said: 'That's the University. It's going to rain tomorrow.' She appeared to be sane. He believed he had understood every word but still had no idea what she meant. Perplexed, he apologized and asked her to repeat what she had said.

► TASK 10

1 What is your first interpretation of the woman's words?
2 What would you need to know about the speaker/the listener/the place/the time, etc., in order to be more certain of building a more accurate mental model?

When she was asked to repeat what she had said, the woman turned her head slightly to one side and pointed her right index finger upwards, at about head height. He interpreted her gesture as meaning 'Listen!' After a second or two, she repeated her comment about the University and the prospect of rain next day. At this point, he realized that the sound she was directing his attention to was that of a bell ringing in the distance. All became clear to him.

► TASK 11

Before reading further, are you now able to construct a fuller, more precise interpretation of the message? If not, what elements in your own mental model still need clarification?

You may still be mystified as to what the woman meant. It was only by going *beyond what she had said* to see what she meant, that her interlocutor was able to reach a satisfactory solution to his comprehension problem. In order to construct an adequate mental model of the intended message, he needed to resort to the following sources of information:

General factual knowledge
1 Sound is more audible downwind than upwind.
2 Wind direction may affect weather conditions.

Local factual knowledge
3 The University of Glasgow has a clock tower with a bell.

Socio-cultural knowledge
4 Strangers in Britain frequently refer to the weather to 'oil the wheels' of social life.
5 A polite comment from a stranger usually requires a response.

Knowledge of context

6 The conversation took place about half a mile from the University of Glasgow.

7 The clock tower bell was just striking the hour.

The example we have used was an extremely brief and linguistically simple conversation. Nevertheless, it was one in which an adult native listener was initially quite unable to comprehend what a well-intentioned, apparently friendly and clear-speaking fellow native speaker had meant, even though he had identified every single word spoken to him.

The division that this example illustrates, between hearing what is said and understanding what is meant, is an extremely important one. Both these aspects of listening—we will call them 'speech perception' and 'interpretation'—are essential parts of the comprehension process. Later, in **2.2**, we will be referring to some research into L1 and L2 speech perception, but for the moment we are concerned with the interpretative part of listening comprehension.

Figure 1 summarizes the relationship between the two principal sources of information we may consult in the process of comprehension. Widdowson (1983) refers to them as (1) *systemic* or linguistic knowledge (knowledge of phonological, syntactic, and semantic components of the language system) and (2) *schematic* or non-linguistic information, which we will shortly discuss further. As we will see in **2**, experimental evidence suggests that we may not distinguish between these information sources in any clear or conscious way. In fact, it is often difficult for us to discriminate between what was actually said and what we have constructed by integrating the spoken words with our own knowledge and experience.

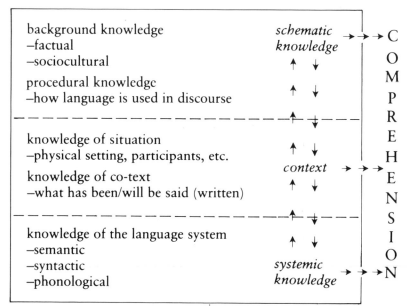

Figure 1: Information sources in comprehension

The term 'schematic' comes from the concept of the schema, associated with the work of the cognitive psychologist Bartlett (1932), which has come into prominence in recent years largely as a result of artificial intelligence research. A schema could be defined as a mental structure, consisting of relevant individual knowledge, memory, and experience, which allows us to incorporate what we learn into what we know. We will briefly mention one area of investigation—the notion of the 'script'— whose findings have special relevance to the process of comprehension, and which we have applied in the construction of our own listening materials (see 7).

Script is the term coined by Schank and Abelson (1977) to describe a set of knowledge of probable sequences of events in familiar situations. Like a film or theatre script, a mental script specifies the roles played by certain actors and the expected sequence of their actions. Unlike the script for a film or play, however, our mental script will not normally specify the precise words that each actor will use.

For instance a 'visiting the dentist' script would contain the actors (patient, receptionist, dentist, nurse) and the events (waiting, examination, treatment) that we associate with such occasions. While those details of the script might well be universal, people from different countries would have differing expectations about, say, how often the visits take place, how long they would have to wait, whether payment is involved, and so on. But the basic script would probably be similar across all cultures where dentistry is a recognized profession.

▶ **TASK 12**

Imagine you meet a friend who has just completed a stay in hospital. When you ask him how it went, he begins his answer with the words 'Fine, except for the visiting hours. They told me I couldn't . . .'

How have you started to interpret his comment? What sort of complaint might he be going to make about the hours? Who do you think he is referring to when he says 'they'? Who are the potential actors in your own hospital script? What are the sources, in your case, for your knowledge or expectations about hospitals?

The idea of the mental script is a powerful one; it offers a plausible explanation of how the mass of memories of individual experience might be organized into networks of connected knowledge. But there is as yet only limited evidence as to how such knowledge can be triggered. Although it is highly unlikely that human listeners/readers operate in exactly the same way as the computer simulations of comprehension that 'scripts' were originally designed for, the general view of listening/reading as a process of model-building, involving active interpretation and the integration of incoming information with prior knowledge and experience, seems to us to be both plausible and fruitful.

It is certainly the most adequate explanation yet available for the relatively complex mental operations that listening requires us to carry out—operations that the 'tape recorder' view of the listener cannot cope with. (For detailed discussion of the role of schematic knowledge in discourse, see Cook: *Discourse*, in this Scheme, and our Further Reading suggestions at the end of the book.)

As teachers, we will not serve our students well if we underestimate the complexity of the listening tasks they face. But by appreciating the range of resources—highlighted by theoretical work of the schema and script type described above—which listeners can draw on in order to listen successfully, we will be in a better position to diagnose the causes of our students' difficulties and to offer appropriate treatment.

1.5 The relationship between listening and speaking

Earlier (in **1.1**) we saw how a carefully prepared L2 utterance is only a useful aid to communication if the speaker can deal effectively with the replies he receives. For the L2 learner to be a proficient partner in conversation, he needs to be skilled as both speaker and listener. However, this interdependence has not always been appreciated by language teachers and course writers, who have often separated off 'listening' and 'speaking' as discrete parts of language competence. Learners need to be given opportunities to practise both sets of skills and to integrate them in conversation. (The need for integrated listening and speaking practice is discussed in detail in Bygate: *Speaking*, in this Scheme.)

The traditional method of developing listening skills—getting learners to listen to a piece of language and then to answer subsequent comprehension questions—has limitations as a technique for developing reciprocal listening skills, partly because it separates the skills of listening and speaking. True, it practises both, but at different stages of the task: speaking is something you do after listening, rather than while you listen.

This sort of listening task also encourages a passive view of listening skills. Since speaking and listening are separated, the listeners are not allowed to interact with the input, i.e. to indicate when there is a comprehension problem, or to provide feedback that they have understood the message. This is likely to lead them to suppose that successful listening is a purely receptive activity in which you merely receive and record what you hear, rather than actively attempt to integrate the incoming information and seek clarification when that interpretation-building process meets an obstacle.

▶ TASK 13

> We could divide real-life listening activities into two simple categories, where you (1) listen without speaking, or (2) listen with the opportunity of speaking. Which of those two types are the following engaged in?
>
> A a student at a lecture
> B someone listening to a radio play
> C pupils being told how to conduct a chemistry experiment
> D someone in lunch-time conversation with a friend
> E a patient listening to his doctor describing a course of treatment.
>
> If the listener has a problem in understanding some part of what he has heard, what can/should he do in each case? Do the sources of help differ in the two categories?
>
> In which category is the responsibility for overcoming any difficulties mainly the listener's, and in which is it the speaker's?

A necessary part of any programme to develop listening skills are tasks that make the relationship between success in listening and speaking clear to the learner. We have already suggested that effective speaking depends on successful listening for L2 learners. In our research with teenage native speakers, we have also found that there is a similar relationship between the two skills. When we conducted communication experiments in which a speaker had to instruct a listener in drawing a diagram or in arranging a set of objects, we found that the most effective spoken performances came from speakers who had previously been listeners on a similar task. Experience as a listener was more beneficial than practice in the speaking role, as it seemed to highlight the needs of the listener for clear and explicit instructions. Many of these native speakers failed to produce 'listener-friendly' messages without prior listening practice (Anderson, Brown, and Yule 1984).

As we will see in 2, children are often less than fully effective speakers of their own language, partly because they do not appreciate their listeners' point of view or current state of knowledge. Moreover, young listeners are not very good at providing the speaker with feedback to indicate a problem in understanding what is being said, and this aggravates the difficulty of communication. A pair of young children (one acting as speaker, the other as listener) may happily continue a communication task, even though the speaker has given quite inadequate instructions. The listener has accepted these without comment or complaint. So for young native speakers, too, there is a clear interrelationship between listening and speaking—one which unfortunately often results in communicative difficulties rather than success.

We discovered similar problems among the teenagers we recorded in our research into success in L1 communication. In paired tasks involving giving and following instructions for marking a route on a map, some speakers produced quite poor performances with vague or inexplicit instructions. The same speakers often seemed to perform unsatisfactorily as listeners, too, ignoring queries or requests for clarification from their partners. So a poor performance from the same instruction-giver often indicated unsuccessful listening and speaking combined. There is a clear inter-dependence between speaking and listening—both within a single speaker/listener and also between partners in a dialogue (see Brown, Anderson, Shadbolt, and Lynch (1987) for details of this experiment).

▶ TASK 14

Here is an invented conversational extract: speaker **A** is a five-year-old and speaker **B** is his grandmother. How do you rate the boy's performance? What factors do you use in forming a judgement?

A: We went to the park, John, Clare, and me, and we bounced and everything.
B: Is Clare in your class at school?
A: We bounced and bounced, then the man said we had to get off.
B: You had to get off? Off what, dear?
A: Bounced and bounced on the bouncy thing, the castle.

If you have identified communication problems, are they due to his ability as speaker or as listener?

An effective programme to develop listening skills has to provide a wide range of listening situations and tasks. Practice in casual conversational listening is one element; what we have called non-reciprocal listening to a text (i.e. where the listeners have no opportunity to intervene when clarification is needed) is another. But relying on only one, or even both, of these—and as we will see in 5, some language courses still provide no other types of practice than these two—leaves a considerable gap in the curriculum. In 7 we will be asking you to assess activities in which listening and speaking are intended to be linked, where the speaking results from the process of following and interpreting listening input.

1.6 The relationship between listening and reading

How the two comprehension skills of listening and reading are related, in L1 and L2 use, is a basic question that researchers have attempted to answer. The traditional view of the relative difficulty of the two activities for native speakers is that listening and oral skills are, under normal circumstances, successfully mastered in the pre-school years, before reading instruction begins. The reading teacher generally concentrates on helping the child to identify the written forms of language—letter, words, sentences, and so on. She assumes that, if the child listened, for example, to a simple story in his first reading book, he would have no difficulty understanding it. He is assumed already to be an effective listener; he can identify sounds and words, he knows how the major part of the syntax of his native language works, and how meanings are conveyed. As a result, little direct attention is paid in schools to the development of listening comprehension skills.

However, the results of recent research challenge this traditional view of the listening/reading relationship. As part of a large-scale L1 survey of 6,000 schoolchildren, Neville (1985) found that they performed very consistently in cloze tests of reading and listening comprehension. At ages 8, 11, and 13 their scores were highly correlated: good listeners were usually good readers and poor listeners were generally poor readers.

Interestingly, there was no evidence of a 'ceiling' effect: in other words, there was no point of maximum success beyond which pupils could not improve. For all the age groups, there was a wide range of scores, with smaller numbers of children performing very poorly at each stage. This suggests that listening is *not* something that we master, once and for all, early on in life. So listening skills may continue to develop over a much longer period than was traditionally believed. Even for native listeners, explicit practice to improve listening skills would be advisable and beneficial, both for its own sake and also as a support to reading skill development.

The same close relationship between reading and listening skills has been observed in groups of relatively poor L1 readers receiving remedial teaching (Carr, Brown, and Vavrus 1985) and in the case of bilinguals (Favreau and Segalowitz 1983). As far as the L2 reading/listening relationship is concerned, the evidence is less clear-cut. Brown and Hayes (1985) found that the relationship held in general, but that one subgroup of the L2 learners they tested—Japanese learners of English—tended to perform better at reading than listening.

► # TASK 15

1 Can you think of possible reasons for the relationship between individuals' L2 reading and listening skills being less clear-cut in the case of adult learners?

2 What might be the particular reasons for Japanese learners giving better performances as readers of English than as listeners to English?

In general, researchers have discovered that there appears to be an important *general language processing skill* that influences performances in both listening and reading. One of the features of this general language processing skill is the ability to monitor your own comprehension of a message. Here there are clear parallels between the problems experienced by listeners and readers.

Markman (1977, 1979) gave young L1 speakers of English deliberately ambiguous or inconsistent messages, orally and in writing. The children were often prepared to claim they understood very ambiguous instructions, without querying them. Similarly, they failed to note apparently obvious inconsistencies in short written texts. They often had problems because they treated each statement in isolation and did not see the texts as a coherent whole.

Garrod (1986) has pointed out that, in both reading and listening, processing has to take place sequentially, i.e. we sample one word at a time. But in order to comprehend the message successfully, we have to analyse whole segments of the input, such as phrases, sentences, and paragraphs. He provides evidence from his own experiments with adult native readers that suggests they do indeed build up an overall interpretation, or 'mental model' (see **1.2**), of a text as they read.

Similar results have been reported from experiments with adult native listeners by Cole and Jakimik (1978, 1980), who found that mispronounced words were spotted more quickly in continuous speech when they occurred in contextually appropriate words. So competent adult L1 readers and listeners do seem to build a global interpretation of what they read or hear, using information from earlier in a text to interpret what they encounter later. The use of such information goes hand-in-hand with the application of schematic knowledge discussed in **1.4**.

Further evidence for the general language processing skill and the particular problem of failure to treat a text as a meaningful whole comes from the types of error reported by Neville (1985) from her reading and listening cloze test. She found that similar kinds of error were made in both types of text and that many mistakes seemed to stem from the reader's or listener's failure to keep the overall content of the text in mind.

▶ # TASK 16

Below are some cloze test items, with invented responses of the sort that might be given by a young native speaker. The correct answer is shown in capital letters at the end of the item; the reader's response is shown in brackets. What is the cause of error in each case?

1 Suddenly the _____ (she) jumped up and ran out of the room.   GIRL

2 John did well at reading and _____ (books).   WRITING.

3 Old Mrs Grant was very poor. She went to the shop and looked in her purse. There were _____ (many) coins inside.   NO

4 The sea-horse swims very slowly. It escapes from its enemies by _____ (rushing) behind rocks.   HIDING.

Do you think that (or do you know whether) adult foreign learners would make similar errors on these items?

Although we know less about the L2 listening/reading relationship, the general pattern seems to be that there is an essential underlying skill of language processing, which includes such elements as the ability to consider each sentence as a complete unit and each text as a unified thematic whole. It appears that proficiency in using this skill is just as important—and difficult—when listening as it is when reading. Developing effective listening skills could well lead not only to improved listening but also to better reading, for foreign learners as well as for native speakers.

2   Listening skills in native speakers

2.1 Introduction

The amount and range of research into the processes of L2 listening comprehension is still very restricted. By focusing on those aspects of listening that cause difficulties even for native listeners, our aim is to provide the language teacher with signposts to areas of listening which are likely to pose problems not only for L1 learners, but for L2 learners as well, and where teaching and practice are likely to be necessary and, we hope, beneficial.

In considering the relationship betwen L1 and L2 listening comprehension, it would be logically possible to maintain any of three positions: (1) that the processes of understanding L1 and L2 speech are quite separate; (2) that they overlap to some extent, or (3) that they are fundamentally the same, apart from specific additional L2 problems. These alternatives are presented in diagrammatic form in Figure 2.

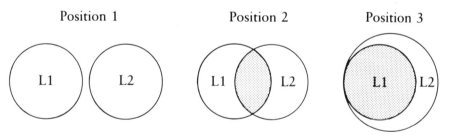

Figure 2: Three views of the relationship between L1 and L2 listening skills

▶   TASK 17

Which of the three views presented in Figure 2 do you think is most appropriate? What evidence do you have, from your experience as an L2 learner/teacher?

As we will see, the available research points to similarities, rather than differences, between L1 and L2 listening comprehension processes. So Position 3 seems to reflect the L1/L2 relationship best. Of course, there *are* aspects of L2 listening that cause different problems, such as those due to the listener's restricted knowledge of vocabulary, but as we will see in **3**, these are often differences of degree, not type.

We begin this part of the book by considering what is involved in the process by which native users listen to and recognize speech. We then provide a selective review of what is known about the development of listening skills in children acquiring their first language, and describe some studies in which researchers have attempted to train young listeners to perform various comprehension tasks more effectively. Finally, we discuss ways in which different types of task and context can influence the ease or success of native listening performance.

2.2 Speech perception

When listening to our native language, we usually do so at speed and without effort. Our attention is focused on the meaning the speaker is trying to convey, rather than on the language (and other) sounds he is producing. Perceiving the speech sounds does not seem problematical, except in unusual circumstances, such as when there is a lot of background noise, or when the speaker has a strong and unfamiliar accent.

Our earlier simple outline of the speech perception process (in **1.1**) was what is known as the 'serial bottom-up' model. It assumed that we perceive speech by building up an interpretation in a series of separate stages, beginning with the lowest-level units (the phonemic segments of words, e.g. /b/, /ɒ/, /g/) and gradually working up to the larger units such as the utterance, from which we then derive our interpretation of the speaker's meaning.

▶ TASK 18

You have just read a summary of the serial bottom-up model of speech perception. An alternative view of listening would be one of a 'top-down' model of comprehension.

What do you think is involved in 'top-down' comprehension? (You might find it helpful to refer back to Figure 1 in **1.4**).

Research has shown that the assumptions in the serial bottom-up model about the nature of spoken language are incorrect: the proposed sequence of independent processing stages is an unworkable representation of the way human beings are able to deal with incoming speech. We will summarize three of the arguments against the serial model:

1 There is no simple one-to-one correspondence between segments of the speech signal and the sounds we perceive. Liberman (1970) showed that if you take a tape recording of a word such as 'bog', it is impossible to cut bits off the tape until all trace of the /b/ has gone and leave a remnant that sounds like 'og'. What remains is in fact unintelligible.

2 For many phonemes there are no unvarying distinctive characteristics that mark them off as absolutely different from all others. The context of the surrounding word affects the phoneme's characteristics.
3 Even at the word level, as opposed to the level of the phoneme, when individual words are extracted from tape recordings of conversations and played for listeners to identify, only about half of the words can be recognized in isolation. If listeners hear them in their original context of utterance, they are readily identified (Pollack and Pickett 1963; Bard and Anderson 1983).

So the quality of spoken signals means that listeners would not be able to perceive speech as successfully as they do if they were in fact engaged in a process of building up the recognition of words *solely* by attempting to identify their constituent phonemes. Adult native listeners do not perceive speech phoneme by phoneme, or word by word. Instead, they use their knowledge of the phonological regularities of their language, its lexicon and its syntactic and semantic properties, to compensate for the shortcomings of the acoustic signal.

In contrast to the serial bottom-up model, this suggests that speech perception is an *interactive process*, so called because we make simultaneous use of a wide variety of information sources and allow the data to 'interact' and produce a known word or phrase (Pollack and Pickett 1963; Marslen-Wilson and Tyler 1980; Elman and McClelland 1984). These sources lie within both the listeners' linguistic or systemic knowledge and also their individual schematic knowledge, discussed in **1.4**.

▶ TASK 19

Which of the following offers L2 learners the most useful description of the listening process?

1 Listening is like reading. If you listen carefully to the individual sounds as if they were letters, then you will be able to recognize the words.

2 When you're listening, the important thing is to recognize each word the speaker says. Take care to hear the words, and the meaning of the sentence will take care of itself.

3 Listening is basically a guessing game. Think about what the speaker is likely to be saying. Try to guess what he means from what you think he would want to communicate.

4 Listening can be hard, so you need all the help you can get. Try to listen carefully to the sounds the speaker produces and at the same time try to use your knowledge of English grammar and vocabulary and your best guess about his intended meaning.

A considerable number of experiments have provided data to support the interactive model of speech perception. Marslen-Wilson (1975) asked people to listen to a message through headphones and to repeat what they heard with as little delay as possible; this sort of task is known as 'speech shadowing'. He found that listeners were able to shadow the recorded message easily and quickly, often lagging behind the message by only one syllable. This suggests that when we listen, we do not need to wait for a word to be completed before we are able to recognize it.

Marslen-Wilson and Welsh (1978) found that listeners shadow normal prose messages more quickly than either (1) syntactically well-formed but meaningless messages, or (2) random sequences of words, which were shadowed with least success of all. So the listening process was more efficient when the listeners could add helpful syntactic and semantic information to the acoustic/phonological information.

It is important to underline the fact the research evidence suggests that *all* available sources of information are used, and probably *simultaneously*. Listeners do not perceive speech by a process of pure—or even educated—guesswork. They do use the acoustic information in the speech signal, but it is often not of sufficient quality to enable them to identify the words spoken if no other information is available. So competent adult L1 listeners exploit all the information they can, to help them to listen successfully and efficiently.

▶ ## TASK 20

If L1 speech perception works through simultaneous use of information from different sources, what type(s) of listening material do you think would be helpful for foreign learners?

1 recordings of 'minimal pairs' (e.g. 'bat' and 'pat' in English) to enable the listeners to build up their ability to discriminate between L2 phonemes

2 lists of isolated words, carefully read by a native speaker

3 a native speaker's instructions to a foreign listener in how to carry out a task, which the learners try to complete themselves

4 a selection of extended extracts from conversations between native speakers

5 recordings of individual grammatically well-formed sentences.

What factors influence your decision?

There have been relatively few studies of L2 speech perception, but two—Voss (1984) and Conrad (1985)—show a similar pattern of results to those in L1 studies. Foreign listeners make similar errors in a task where they have to transcribe a tape-recorded text, and many of the errors show that, unless they are beginners, L2 listeners process incoming speech in meaningful 'chunks'. They use higher-level information, such as expectations about meaning, to supplement the acoustic/phonological information, rather than relying solely on identifying sounds and words one by one.

2.3 The acquisition of listening skills in childhood

So far, we have focused our discussion of what successful listening might be like on the behaviour of adult listeners. How then, as babies and children, do we learn to listen to our own language effectively? We are listeners long before we are speakers. Babies as young as three days old have been shown to prefer listening to speech to listening to other sounds (Butterfield and Siperstein 1974). By about eight weeks they have developed some sensitivity as listeners, being able to distinguish the emotional qualities of voice: they respond differently to angry voices, which tend to make them cry, and to friendly ones, which produce smiles and coos (Kaplan and Kaplan 1970). By four months they seem to differentiate male and female voices, and by six to eight months, it is claimed, they can imitate the intonation pattern of speech addressed to them and are able to distinguish the intonation of statements and questions (Nakazima 1962; Kaplan 1969).

Most babies gain their first experience of being a listener through their participation in 'conversations' with their parents. These begin long before the baby is able to participate by speaking. Instead, the doting parents respond to a wide range of non-linguistic behaviours as if these were the baby's replies or conversational turns. Perfectly rational adults treat yawns, burps, smiles, or gestures as expressions of interest or comments on the current topic of conversation (Snow 1977). As the baby grows older, the adults become more demanding about what they will accept as an appropriate conversational response. So at three months almost any physical sign of interest or attention will do, but by eight months a vocal response such as babbling is usually required; by the time the child is one year old he or she is expected to produce a word in response to the parent's prompting.

► TASK 21

> What do you think parents believe they are doing when they engage in 'conversation' with children before they can speak? What do you think is happening in these conversations, from the baby's point of view?

It is believed that this parental behaviour is an unconscious attempt to provide the baby with training in the art of conversation. Children are presented with many opportunities to absorb what is expected of speakers and listeners, even before they are able to produce the required response. By the time they can really talk, they have already assimilated many of the basic conversational skills, such as paying attention to the listener, attracting the listener's attention, and taking turns to speak. Children as young as two years old display some of the relevant listener skills in conversation with adults. For example, they reply to the adults' questions about 80 per cent of the time (Gallagher 1977). However, when the content of their responses is analysed, they show themselves to be less than fully proficient, e.g. they may recognize that a 'yes/no' question demands a response, but the semantic content of that reply may be questionable (Steffenson 1978; Horgan 1978).

▶   TASK 22

Which type of skill does the child master earlier?

1 social skills, concerned with maintaining friendly interaction with the interlocutor

2 cognitive skills, concerned with the efficient transfer of information between speaker and listener.

Research into children's conversational skills highlights those listener skills which very young children have not yet fully mastered, but also indicates the considerable abilities they do possess, particularly in the social aspects of listening. So, although two-year-olds have been found to be imperfect turn-takers (for example, leaving excessively long gaps between speaking turns), by the age of five or six some children can explicitly discuss turn-taking and attempt to remedy overlapping speech in a conversation by stopping and remembering what they want to say while simultaneously monitoring others' ongoing talk (Ervin-Tripp 1979). Listeners as young as two years old have been found to be quite competent in their interpretation of indirect as well as direct requests from their mothers (Shatz 1978). The picture that emerges from such studies is that, in spontaneous conversation in a familiar context, usually with a familiar partner, young native listeners demonstrate a quite considerable range of communicative competence.

One characteristic of such studies is that the *information content* of the listening material is not very demanding—which is hardly surprising, since this is the norm for casual conversations, even among adults, as shown in 1. However, it is important to bear it in mind when we consider the results of another type of research, which has focused on the listener's ability to deal effectively with inputs that are novel and informative, rather than familiar and interactional. This kind of input demands the deployment of skills that are less social than cognitive. Although the experiments which focus on novel and informative inputs may seem less 'natural' than those concerned in the familiar and interactional kinds, they tap abilities which are just as essential for complete competence, and which the adult native listener needs to have mastered.

Researchers have used a technique known as the 'referential communication paradigm' to study how well young listeners (and speakers) cope with the information content of messages. The children are given a task that involves the speaker looking at a set of cards with simple pictures or diagrams, one of which is marked as the 'target'. The speaker has to give a clear enough description to enable the hearer, who has an identical set of cards, to identify the target from the unmarked set.

▶ ## TASK 23

1 How does the 'referential communication paradigm' differ from the other research into children's communicative skills that we have described so far?

2 What types of skill are involved in giving an effective performance on this task?

Three ways in which *listeners* can aid successful communication in referential tasks have been suggested (Glucksberg, Kraus, and Higgins 1975). First, they have to judge their confidence in having understood what the speaker has said; in other words, they need to be able to *recognize* ambiguous or uninformative messages. Second, if they identify just such a problem, they have to be able to *inform* the speaker about the difficulty. Third, they should be able to *specify* what additional or alternative information the speaker should supply in order to clarify the message.

Recent research has emphasized the importance of the listener's contribution to communicative success and has highlighted the problems faced by young listeners. These have been shown to be of three main types:

1 Many children (up to the age of seven) *do not realize the importance of message quality*. In referential tasks the listeners blame themselves, rather than the quality of the message, even if this was highly ambiguous. Similarly, when asked to judge message quality, young listeners are misled by the outcome; if they have guessed correctly, they think that even an ambiguous message was adequate. They maintain this view, even when the experimenter stresses the fact that they have guessed. By the age of eight, most children have overcome these difficulties (Robinson and Robinson 1977a, 1977b; Singer and Flavell 1981).

2 Young listeners *have problems assessing message quality*, that is, recognizing when input is ambiguous or uninformative, as we saw in Markman's research (1.5). Asher (1976) found that seven-year-old listeners judged four out of six adequate messages correctly, but noticed only one third of the inadequate ones. Even eleven-year-olds found such judgements difficult: although by this age all the adequate messages were correctly assessed, still about one third of the ambiguous items were judged to be satisfactory.

3 Unlike adults, young listeners *rarely provide feedback for speakers*. In spontaneous conversation and in communication tasks, children do not usually confirm that they have understood when the message is clear and simple. More seriously, even when a speaker's message is highly ambiguous or unclear, young listeners (up to the age of ten or eleven) also fail to comment, query, or request more information (Dittman

1972; Cosgrove and Patterson 1977; Ironsmith and Whitehurst 1978; Patterson and Kister 1981).

▶ TASK 24

Why do you think young listeners tend to provide no feedback for the speaker when (1) communication is progressing smoothly, and (2) a problem arises?

These studies of how young children perform in the role of listener have provided valuable insights into the wide range of component skills involved in effective listening. In supportive and familiar conversational contexts even very young listeners are competent in the social skills involved in listening. Experimental research has now focused more on the difficulties experienced by the child when faced with more novel, information-oriented listening tasks. In both these types of study, we see that there is a gradual developmental progression towards competent listening performances. The age at which this competence is achieved varies with the difficulty of the listening task. Task difficulty is a constant and critical feature of all these studies and is an issue we return to in **2.5**. Notice that by the age of six or seven young native speakers have a fair mastery of language, but they are less than effective *communicators*. This is partly because their listening skills are not yet fully developed. Their linguistic competence does not automatically lead to successful listening or communication.

2.4 Developing listening skills in young native speakers

We have seen that although children master many aspects of listening at an early age, several sorts of listening task cause difficulty throughout childhood, especially when they involve monitoring for the adequacy of information. As the skills involved here are predominantly cognitive rather than social, it is to these information-processing skills that training studies have mainly been directed, in an attempt to elicit more effective performances from young listeners. Most have used the referential communication paradigm, described in **2.3**, which allows the accuracy of the listener's performance to be assessed objectively, as well as the adequacy of the speaker's message.

Training studies have been carried out with young listeners between the ages of four and ten, who have been found to perform more effectively after training that stressed the importance of asking the speaker for more information when the message is inadequate (Cosgrove and Patterson 1977). Similar improvements have been shown when children have previously watched 'model' videotaped performances, in which adult listeners ask for information to supplement inadequate messages (Ironsmith and Whitehurst 1978). But in both studies the youngest listeners (aged four to five) showed no improvement, unlike older children.

▶ TASK 25

It appears that four and five-year-olds do not benefit from training in question-asking, in the way that listeners of eight or nine do. What are the possible reasons for the difference in the effectiveness of such training for the two groups?

You might consider differences in:

1 memory
2 ability to form questions
3 status

Are there any other differences that could be influential?

Another technique which has proved effective in improving communication skills is the provision of explicit feedback about message quality. Robinson (1981) described one such study with children who were 'listener-blamers'. These are the young children of four and five, mentioned in 2.2, who seem to lack an appreciation of the role of message quality and who blame the listener for communication failures, even when the speaker's message is extremely ambiguous.

In the experiment, children of five and six took the speaker's role in a communication game with an adult listener. One group of children were given explicit feedback by the adult on all the ambiguous messages they produced; she then elicited a more adequate message from them, before making her choice of target. Before and after this task, the children were tested for their appreciation of the role of message quality. In the post-training task, most of the children who had been listener-blamers before training, but who had been given feedback during their communication task, now correctly blamed the quality of the message when asked to assign blame for a communication failure. Very few of the untrained children changed their false assumption that such failures were always the fault of the listener, even when the message was ambiguous.

▶ TASK 26

Here is an invented exchange from a communication experiment. **A** and **B** both have three cards: the first shows a blue star, the second a red circle, and the third a blue circle. **A** is the 'speaker' and her blue circle is marked as the target. **B**, as 'listener', has unmarked cards.

A: It's the blue one.
B: Right, I've got it. (*He picks the blue star.*)

1 Imagine that **A** and **B** are five years old. If you asked **A** whose fault it was that they made a mistake, who would she blame? Who would **B** blame?

2 How might their feelings about blame be different at the age of eight?

It appears that the mastery of several listening skills can be accelerated or facilitated by appropriate training. Providing model performances of successful listening and providing a plan of what is required of the listener when problems occur are both effective when the input material is fairly restricted, as in the typical experimental study using pictures or simple diagrams. With more complex input, success has been achieved by combining training in comparison and self-evaluation.

The successful methods seem to depend on the listener already possessing the requisite skills, but not realizing their relevance to the current listening task. Some of the methods have proved less effective with the youngest listeners tested. This may be because more fundamental listening skills were not yet mastered, such as an appreciation of the role of message quality, or an ability to make appropriate comparisons, or to formulate specific relevant requests to the speaker for clarification.

2.5 The influence of task and context

In everyday life we listen in a host of different situations for a wide range of purposes. We therefore set ourselves different listening tasks in different contexts. On one occasion we might judge a speaker's emotional state from their tone of voice; we could find ourselves trying to decide, for example, whether a remark such as 'I was a bit surprised by your phone call' means just that, or indicates that the speaker was in fact angry, shocked, or disappointed. Presumably this kind of listening is fairly automatic and not very difficult—at least for the mature native listener.

Sometimes the same spoken input will be used for very different purposes by different listeners. For instance, two people might be waiting outside an office door before going in to see a third person who can be heard talking on the telephone. One may only be trying to monitor when the call has ended; the other, convinced he is the topic of the telephone conversation, might be straining to catch every word and trying to reconstruct the whole conversation from the one side he can hear. Obviously, the second person has set himself a much more demanding listening task.

So we can vary the type of information we try to extract from any input; similarly, we can vary the amount of material we attempt to process in any particular message. We may select this chosen material on the grounds of importance, relevance, or personal interest. In addition, we are able to 'half-listen'—to the radio, for example—and to decide whether a particular item might become interesting or significant to us in some way. So we have the ability to 'change our minds' as listeners; we can alter our chosen listening purpose in mid-task, as it were, although probably not all such 'decisions' are taken as a result of conscious attention. These are formidable skills which we normally take for granted and which are not well understood by researchers.

▶ TASK 27

What kind of task are the listeners in these situations likely to attempt?

1 a television programme producer interviewing candidates for a job as a newsreader

2 a detective interrogating a suspected burglar

3 a motorist about to set off on a long winter journey, listening to the news on the radio

4 a journalist listening to the same radio news

5 a doctor listening to a patient who has complained of a sore throat

Is it the listener or the input that is more important in determining the listening task? Or a combination of the two? What other factors might be important?

We have considered the way in which listeners may unconsciously alter the listening task for themselves. Successful listeners can, of course, also adapt their mode of listening consciously or in response to specific instructions. Similarly, in an educational or experimental setting, fully competent listeners can complete specified comprehension tasks, such as listening for the main points of a tape-recorded discussion, listening in order to retell a story to a third person, or following spoken instructions on how to assemble a piece of equipment. In performing these tasks, they are able to vary their listening behaviour appropriately.

However, not all listeners are able to change their listening in this way. In our own research with teenage L1 listeners, we conducted one study (Brown, Anderson, Shadbolt, and Lynch 1987) where listeners heard short passages through headphones and then had to relay as much of the text as possible to a partner. The passages were replayed and the same listeners were then asked to give a very brief summary of the text, including only essential details. Many listeners found it very hard to switch listening task in this way; they produced 'summaries' that were as long as, or longer than, their original 'comprehensive' versions.

As far as we are aware, no researchers have specifically investigated the problems faced by foreign listeners when trying to respond flexibly to different tasks in different listening contexts. We would assume that the ability to switch listening tactics to match a particular situation is a relatively advanced skill, but also an essential one. In our present state of knowledge, how best to train listeners flexibly to alter listening mode—consciously or unconsciously—in response to different listening demands is still very much an open question.

3 Listening skills in foreign learners

3.1 Introduction

There is relatively little research which provides a description of the listening skills of foreign learners, or of the problems they experience in learning to listen to the L2. That is why in earlier sections we have referred to some of the L1 research that might offer us useful guidance as teachers on the kind of difficulty our students might experience in the process of listening itself. However, for foreign listeners, there are of course additional problems associated with trying to understand a language in which they are only partially proficient (see Figure 2). In **3.4** and **3.5** below, we outline what these language problems might be and how closely they relate to the problems of listening in general. But first we will look briefly at the overall relationship between comprehension and learning.

3.2 The role of comprehension in L2 learning

The role played by comprehension in L2 learning has come under close scrutiny in recent years from researchers interested in wider issues than simply listening skills. Among others, Krashen (e.g. 1981) has claimed that comprehension plays a central—and possibly predominant part—in the whole process of language learning. In this book we are concerned with ways in which teachers might facilitate learners' ability to understand language in context, rather than with the fundamental issues of whether/how/when short-term comprehension leads to long-term learning. However, we think it would be useful at least to summarize the main issues, as background to the discussion on listening skills in L2 learners.

Current approaches to the role of listening comprehension have their roots in the observation of two essential features of L1 acquisition. First, young children are typically allowed a '*silent period*' in the early part of their lives, during which they are not expected to attempt to produce adult-like language in response to input addressed to them. Second, even after they have begun to attempt linguistic production, children clearly *understand more than they can say*.

The recognition of these characteristics of the L1 acquisition context has had a major influence on at least two areas of L2 learning/teaching research. First, it led to the development of a variety of teaching methods known collectively as the 'Comprehension Approach', the most widely-known of which is Total Physical Response. (For a comprehensive survey of this approach, see Winitz 1981).

What the various forms of the Comprehension Approach have in common is a concentration, in the beginner phase of a language course, on activities that develop the learners' comprehension, without requiring them to produce the L2; they respond either in a non-verbal way (performing physical actions or marking worksheets, for example) or they might answer in their L1. Practitioners of the various methods claim that relieving the learners of the burden of speaking the L2 before they feel ready to leads to increased confidence, motivation, and competence, compared to that of students taught conventionally.

▶   TASK 28

What is your reaction to the claim that L2 learners feel that having to speak the target language is a 'burden' in the early stage of their learning?

Think about your own experience as learner and teacher, and consider what factors might cause the beginner stress when asked to produce the L2.

The second area of influence on research into the characteristics of the language environment for L1 acquisition has been the growth of interest in the relationship between the language that the L2 learner is exposed to, inside and/or outside the classroom, and his own developing language competence. The key term in this connection is *comprehensible input*. So far in this book we have been using the word 'input' to describe all the incoming speech (and other) signals that listeners hear, and from which they select cues in order to construct a mental model of the speaker's message. Such input is, so to speak, input-for-comprehension.

But at least some parts of what a language learner hears (or reads) may also function as input-for-learning. In other words, it may serve as a basis for the learning of a new form of language, or a new use of a familiar form:

> . . . comprehension may be at the heart of the language acquisition process: perhaps we acquire by *understanding* language that is 'a little beyond' our current level of competence. This is done with the aid of extra-linguistic context and our knowledge of the world.
> (*Krashen 1981: 102*)

Clearly, 'comprehensible input' is essential when we learn a foreign language; it would be unlikely that we could learn without understanding. But what remains unclear—and is still very much in dispute (e.g. Swain 1985; Faerch and Kasper 1986)—are the conditions under which the same input may operate in two ways, (1) as input-for-comprehension and (2) as input-for-learning. But precisely how these two operations are linked or distinct is not yet established and the issue remains open to research (see Sharwood Smith 1986, for discussion).

▶ TASK 29

Think of situations in which you can recall having learnt L2 words or expressions by hearing them used. Can you remember what it was about the item or the context that enabled you to learn and remember? If possible, ask colleagues and friends to give you their answers to this question.

In an analysis of the input conditions that might help to promote learning Faerch and Kasper (1986) came to the conclusion—a particularly interesting one for the focus of this book—that 'if input is to function as intake to the learning of higher-level L2 material, *learners need to experience comprehension problems*' (1986: 270, our emphasis). They suggest that it is only by working on the problems that arise in trying to understand a sample of L2 input that learners become aware of gaps in their internal L2 systems. Given certain conditions, they will attempt to fill in that gap, i.e. learn. We will now be considering in more detail the nature and extent of these potentially fruitful comprehension problems for L2 learners and later (in 7) we discuss their exploitation in our own listening comprehension materials.

3.3 Background problems

The obvious answer to the question 'What causes the comprehension problems that foreign learners have and native speakers don't?' is 'the language'. But this really only scratches the surface. It makes two assumptions: (1) that what L2 learners are doing is learning a *language* and no more; (2) that native speakers do not experience comprehension problems comparable with those of L2 listeners. Both assumptions need to be questioned.

Let us take the first assumption. When we learn a foreign language, we do more than learn a linguistic system, we acquire some degree of familiarity with the foreign cultural system. Language is the means used by a community to express facts, ideas, beliefs, rules, and so on—in short, to express its culture. So gaps in our knowledge of the L2 culture, of the associations and references available to native users, can present obstacles to comprehension.

▶ TASK 30

Here are three spoken headlines from the BBC 1 *Six O'Clock News* of 26 November 1986:

1 'If you drink and drive, you're a menace'—the Government's message this Christmas.

2 Higgins is told 'Play on for the moment'. Police are investigating allegations of assault.

3 President Reagan's Attorney General says he believes more people could be involved in the arms scandal.

Which took longest to understand? Why? What did you need to do in order to interpret the meanings?

Secondly, L2 learners underestimate the native user's comprehension problems. Although foreign learners are naturally only too aware of their own misunderstandings of the L2, it is also the case that native users of the same language may fail to understand each other. The example of the Glaswegian's comment about the university and rain (1.4) shows how misunderstandings can arise if a speaker wrongly assumes that the listener shares their background knowledge.

Equally, what works as perfectly adequate communication for the people involved may be incomprehensible to an eavesdropper who happens to be an outsider, either in terms of language or culture. We will illustrate this point with a short conversational extract, based on real life. You are unlikely to find any words in it that you have not encountered before, whether you are a native reader of English or not; but the meaning may well remain unclear, if you are an outsider to the sub-culture relevant to the conversation.

▶ TASK 31

Please follow these instructions exactly. Take a piece of paper and cover up the whole extract below. Then read it slowly and carefully, uncovering only a single line at a time. After each of speaker **B**'s turns, make a note of what you think **A** and **B** are talking about. All you need to know at this stage is that they are colleagues at work.

A: What's it like, then?
B: Not bàd. It's got a good short menu, which saves quite a bit of time.
A: It doesn't have a mouse, does it?
B: No, not at that price, no.
A: Anything else special?
B: Well, it's got a thing to stop you having to worry about widows and orphans.
A: So you're happy with it, then?
B: So far, yes.
A: Did you get the 512, in the end?
B: No, the 256.

In that particular case the words 'menu', 'mouse', 'widow', and 'orphan' are unlikely to have been new to you. But you may have been unfamiliar with their specialized meanings in the context of the topic that **A** and **B** were discussing: features of a word processor that **A** knew **B** had recently bought. So one source of misunderstanding or non-comprehension, for both native and foreign readers and listeners, may be the unfamiliar use of a familiar word or phrase.

As we saw in **1.4**, background knowledge is crucial to the way we understand language. It is often the absence or incompleteness of such information that results in the sort of non-comprehension that the foreign listener experiences: where the language element in fact presents no obstacle, but where it is the lack of shared schematic or contextual information that makes comprehension difficult or impossible. In 7 we will come back to the importance of the role played by information sources other than language when we discuss classroom studies in which L1 and L2 learners worked on identical listening comprehension tasks.

3.4 Language problems

Although we have said that the L2 language system may not always be the principal cause of comprehension difficulty, the L2 learner will still come up against problems that are primarily linguistic. It is reasonable to assume that the foreign listener will have particular problems when the language input is difficult, but the question arises: what do we actually mean by 'difficult' input?

One seemingly obvious way in which input can be more or less complex is in terms of its syntactic structure. It was this aspect of language comprehension that was the subject of psycholinguistic research in the 1960s and early 1970s, in studies which tested a range of grammatical structures within single sentences to see how easily they could be understood. Studies were carried out with L1 listeners (adults and children) and adult L2 learners in understanding particular syntactic forms. Various forms that caused difficulty for young native speakers were also often misinterpreted by lower-level L2 learners. Older L1 listeners and more advanced L2 learners had no such problem. So it seems that input which is syntactically difficult for young children causes comparable problems for older foreign learners, who—in the initial stages of L2 learning—appear not to benefit from their L1 experience of similarly difficult surface structures (Cook 1973; d'Anglejan and Tucker 1975).

Although this type of research has produced interesting data, it does not deal with listening/reading in a natural context. The problems experienced by learners when coping with single sentences without a meaningful context may not throw much light on the difficulties the listener faces outside the laboratory. As we saw in **1.6**, researchers studying the listening or reading behaviour of adult native speakers now generally accept that a whole range of information sources are used simultaneously.

Rather than continuing to study particular structures (or vocabulary) that give problems when presented in isolation, it might be better to consider other questions. For example, are there tactics that L2 learners could adopt to overcome their language disadvantages? More generally, are they in fact likely to encounter such syntactic complexities in the early stages of language learning? These are the questions that we try to answer here and in **3.5**.

Let us first consider the type of language to which the learner is likely to be exposed, both in formal teaching and in informal learning outside the classroom, such as in conversation with native speakers. Reviewing research into informal conversations between native speakers and child L2 learners, Hatch, Peck, and Wagner-Gough (1979) note three central features of the language produced for foreign listeners. First, the L2 learners are exposed to a *restricted set of grammatical structures*. Second, the conversations provide the listeners with *repeated exposure* to fairly large chunks of language. Third—particularly during play—the child learners receive input that is both *well contextualized and predictable*, with the speaker often referring to the immediate context, the 'here-and-now', and using accompanying gestures to help to make the meaning clear.

▶ ## TASK 32

Extracts A and B come from a study of L2 listeners' comprehension of native speakers' modifications (see Lynch 1988a). In each case, the same native speaker is giving instructions for a communication game. Her partners are a fellow native speaker (Extract A) and an adult elementary EFL learner (Extract B).

Extract A
'your task is to + number the pictures in the story + in the right order + . . . you have a jumbled order'

Extract B
'you have some pictures + and you have to put the pictures in the right order + and you have to write number one + by the picture you think is the first picture in the story + and number two + by the picture you think is the second picture in the story + and so on until number six + and there are six pictures'

Which of the three features identified by Hatch, Peck, and Wagner-Gough (above) does this native speaker use to the L2 listener?

(Here, and in transcript extracts elsewhere in the book, a plus sign (+) is used to indicate a pause.)

In **2** we stressed the importance of the listener's active participation in conversation, signalling when they are having problems of comprehension; we saw how it is a skill that young native listeners have to acquire and develop. The same holds for L2 learners. In an analysis of interaction between older L2 learners and native speakers, Hatch (1978) considered the effects such signals had on the input they received from their native partners. She noted a variety of types of clarification on the part of the native speakers. For instance, they may alter the words used to describe the topic, so that vocabulary in the reformulated utterance may be more specific or more common. So in real-life L2 learning situations the foreign learner can to some extent get the language input tailored to his particular needs, by indicating when he cannot understand what has been said. In this way, he may succeed in eliciting a modified version of the utterance which is 'simpler' in one of a number of ways.

▶ TASK 33

Look at these two extracts from conversations between a teenager in the early stages of learning English and a native speaker (from Butterworth 1972). How does the native speaker attempt to respond when the learner indicates he is having problems?

Extract A
NS: Do you wear them every day?
L: Huh?
NS: Do you put them on every day?
L: Wear?
NS: Yeah do you (*gesture*) put them on every day?
L: Ah! No *muy* . . .

Extract B
NS: Did you have a nice weekend?
L: Huh?
NS: Friday, Saturday . . . did you have fun?

The nature of the input and interaction modifications that occur in native/non-native interaction has been extensively investigated over the last fifteen years or so. However, as far as our own interest is concerned, the studies have a basic weakness: very few actually approach native/non-native conversations from the point of view of the L2 listener. Most researchers have focused on what *native speakers* '*do*', as opposed to whether or how much *foreign learners understand* as a result.

This is surprising. Since a major reason for studying native/non-native interaction at all is to see how the two partners collaborate to produce 'comprehensible input', it would seem logical to investigate the extent to which the various types of modification actually help the L2 listener to cope. Here, as in other areas of L2 research, (cf. Faerch and Kasper

1983) the bias is towards the analysis of production rather than comprehension.

The comparatively few studies that do analyse the effects of language
modification on the L2 listener's success in understanding—reviewed by
Chaudron (1985)—all report the results of controlled experiments with
non-reciprocal listening tasks, using scripted or semi-scripted recordings
such as mini-lectures and dictations. There seems to have been very little
published research into what is termed 'on-line comprehension', i.e.
situations in which listeners have to understand speech addressed to them
at the time they have to react to it.

▶ TASK 34

You have just read a definition of 'on-line comprehension'. Think of
examples of comprehension tasks that could be described as
'off-line'.

From the L2 learners' point of view, which type of comprehension is
more demanding? Which type do they get more opportunity to
practise in the L2 classroom?

3.5 Listening problems

L1 and L2 comprehension studies have tended to focus on syntactic issues,
concentrating on the problems presented by the language rather than on
the processes of comprehension. But one branch of second language
acquisition research has given more explicit consideration to what is
involved in L2 listening processes: *discourse analysis studies* have
examined how L2 learners cope when conversing with native speakers.

One of the principal skills which listeners must develop if they are to
participate successfully in conversation is the ability *to identify the topic of
conversation*, so that they can make a relevant response. In the early stages
of language learning, identifying the topic accurately enough to make an
immediate relevant reply is apparently a very hard task. This was one of the
conclusions drawn by Hatch (1978) in a large-scale research study of the
conversations of both child and adult L2 learners with native speakers.

▶ TASK 35

Look back to our earlier discussion of the role of schematic
knowledge (in **1.4**). What advantages are there for the L2 listener in
being able to recognize the speaker's topic?

To get clarification of a topic, foreign learners have to develop strategies to
make their difficulties plain to their native partner. This essential
conversational skill is, of course, one that we also use in our L1, though less

frequently than in an L2. (For further discussion of its role in the development of L2 conversational skills, see Bygate 1987).

Hatch illustrated how learners dealt with this problem of topic clarification by using stock responses, such as 'huh?', 'excuse me?' or 'I don't understand', or by echoing part of the preceding utterance, as indications that the learner is having difficulties in knowing how to respond. The importance of such strategies in getting a simpler or alternative formulation of the topic from the native speaker was strikingly demonstrated in a telephone exercise. When foreign listeners did not make use of these responses, the native speakers they were calling hung up more frequently before the learners had achieved their aim in making the call; when learners persevered and kept showing that they were trying, but having problems, the native speakers were more willing to let the call continue.

Hatch's conclusion was that we might need to reconsider the traditional view of what it is the foreign listener has to do in listening comprehension, at least in the case of face-to-face conversation. The successful (lower-level) L2 listener does not seem to proceed by finely discriminating between all the phonological, syntactic, and semantic information in the native's speech, as some conventional approaches to training listening would seem to assume. This supports the view of L1 and L2 speech perception processes presented in 2.2.

▶   TASK 36

Below is an extract from Hatch's data: it shows a conversation between a native speaker (NS) and a foreign learner (NNS). The learner's task is to arrange for the native speaker to type a thesis. As you read it, think about the sources of information the listener is using as the basis for each response.

1 Find examples where the foreign listener seems to:
  − use her general understanding of the topic of conversation as the basis for her response
  − process one or two key words in the speaker's utterance and reply according to her prediction of what the rest of the utterance might have been
  − make immediately relevant responses.

NS: Which University is it for?
NNS: Yes I have a more 100
NS: Pardon me?
NNS: I have more 100 page
NS: Yes but is it for UCLA? or USC?
NNS: UCLA
NS: I see well is it typed?
NNS: Type? Yes uh for the I don't I don't type

NS: Is it handwritten?
NNS: Uh pardon me? Excuse me?
NS: Is your thesis handwritten?
NNS: I don't understand you. Because excuse me I I speak a little
        bit English. I speak French. Do you speak French?
NS: No unfortunately not enough. No I know a very little but I
        really couldn't speak it. Mmm is your thesis now typewritten
        or did you write it by hand?
NS: Ah yes by hand
(*Hatch 1978: 416–17*)

2 How many times in this short extract does the learner signal
   comprehension problems?

3 What effect do these signals have on the native speaker?

Three main skills emerge from the discourse analysis studies as being of
prime importance for the L2 listener:

1 the ability to recognize the topic of conversation from the native
   speaker's initial remarks

2 the ability to make predictions about likely developments of the topic to
   which he will have to respond

3 the ability to recognize and signal when he has not understood enough of
   the input to make a prediction or a response. These explicit signals are
   crucial, as they usually elicit a repetition or reformulation by the native
   speaker, and so give the listener another chance to make a relevant
   response.

In using these skills, the listener may exploit any or all of the various
information sources illustrated in Figure 1 (in **1.4**). The implication for
developing the skills necessary for successful L2 listening which emerges
from a wide range of research studies in L1 and L2 contexts is that teaching
programmes should not over-emphasize comprehension as a process of
identifying sounds and matching them against the learners' store of known
words. Not only is this not all that native speakers or proficient L2 learners
do when they listen, but such an acoustically-based approach is likely to
handicap, rather than help, elementary-level L2 learners.

Especially in the early stages of L2 learning, learners need to utilize the
other types of data discussed in **1.4** (knowledge of discourse content, of the
context, and any available knowledge of the L2 linguistic system, e.g. its
grammar) to help them make predictions about the identity of incoming
words, so as to make up for their natural shortcomings in acoustic
processing.

The importance of guiding and encouraging L2 learners to realize the
extent to which they can, as it were, *help themselves to understand* by using
their own internal knowledge resources when they have problems in

processing incoming spoken language is something that has recently been stressed by Faerch and Kasper (1986) and Garrod (1986). In particular, Faerch and Kasper make the following claim:

> Even though some low-level processing will take place in any comprehension task, the decisive operations in comprehension for communication (rather than in laboratory experiments) involve higher-level processes of meaning reconstruction.
> (*Faerch and Kasper 1986: 264*)

This is a bold claim, and perhaps an overstatement, in the present state of research. However, we would agree that in the past these higher-level processes have been somewhat neglected in the language classroom. In 7 we present some results of our classroom-based research, which lend support to the idea that language teachers should be helping listeners by encouraging them to use their internal resources as a support in listening.

4 Graded development of listening skills

4.1 Introduction

Any programme intended to teach either an area of knowledge or a skill must involve the principled selection and ordering of materials or activities. Learners should be encouraged by achieving success on less complex tasks before moving to the more complex. In language teaching this can only be brought about if they begin by receiving or producing a restricted or simplified sample of the language, or have to perform limited or simple tasks.

This seems obvious when we consider L2 productive skills: as teachers, we do not expect beginners to start by producing extended discourse on abstract topics with complex structures. When we first require them to speak, we expect them to begin with short, simple utterances in a supportive context. When developing learners' comprehension, the principle of grading is just as important, but—as we will see in 6—it is sometimes neglected. In 7 we explain how we have used the findings of experimental research to grade the level of difficulty of listening tasks.

▶ TASK 37

> We have suggested that grading should be an integral part of language teaching programmes. Presenting learners with a gradual increase in difficulty is likely to raise their motivation. Can you suggest other reasons why grading is (or is not) appropriate in the specific case of listening comprehension?

There are a number of reasons why easier tasks should be tackled before more difficult ones. As we have already said, the learners' motivation is one important factor. We know that in learning to speak a foreign language, the *confidence* to begin and sustain a conversation, however inaccurately, is a crucial factor in the development of *competence* in speaking skills. Similarly, in listening, success depends in part on the learners' active participation: having the confidence to ask for clarification or repetition when the opportunity arises. A listener who has experienced success in simple comprehension tasks is more likely to have the necessary self-confidence to adopt these active listening tactics. In contrast, if learners have been exposed to listening materials that are so difficult as to be incomprehensible, they suffer in two ways: not only is the whole experience a dispiriting one, but it is also likely to encourage passive and unsuccessful listening habits where the learners equate 'listening' with sitting back and letting a largely meaningless sequence of sounds wash over them.

Another major advantage of a graded approach to listening training is that it provides a way of dealing with the complexities of language input. In any piece of real language there are a number of features—or variables—that potentially make the language more or less difficult for the listener. (We will examine what some of these might be in **4.3** and **4.4**). It is probably impossible, therefore, to control and grade all the features of a specific language text. But if we are able to identify one or two variables that may be of particular importance as potential sources of listening difficulty, and assess the text as relatively simple in terms of those features, then listeners stand a better chance of dealing with any unforeseen complexities in *other features* of the input than they would if all the features of a text vary randomly.

▶ TASK 38

You want to give an intermediate-level L2 group practice in listening to stories and in understanding descriptions of characters' feelings. You have decided to play a story and then ask the students to discuss what emotions the main character experienced and why. Here is a summary of two recordings you have available. Which story would you use first? Why?

Story 1
This story involves the Bruce family—mother, father, and three teenage children—over a one-week period at home, at work, and at school. Mum starts the week depressed because everybody takes her for granted. Gradually the family realize how much she does for them all and by the weekend she is happy again.

Story 2
This is about one Saturday in the life of Tom and Kate, a recently married couple in their new home. Kate starts off very worried because she cannot cope with all she has to do as a working wife, but over the day Tom sees she is unhappy. They divide the housework and that makes both of them happy.

Assume that both stories are three minutes long and would present few vocabulary problems to the students.

Our overall view of listening, based on general psychological models, is that the human listener is a 'limited processor'. Each of us has a certain fixed amount of information processing capacity available to us. The more processing capacity that is used up in dealing with complexities of dimension A, the less is available for interpreting dimension B. So when A requires less effort to understand, then more mental resources can be devoted to coping with B.

So, in Task 38, understanding the description of the characters' emotions may seem a relatively difficult aspect of the task. But once this has been accomplished in a text that is simple on other dimensions (e.g. number of characters, shifts of time and location), this feature can then be tackled in more complex texts with greater likelihood of success, due to the listeners' practice with and experience of the simple narrative.

4.2 What makes listening easy or difficult?

Everyday experience tells us that listening is sometimes hard and sometimes easy, but we are normally unaware which factors are contributing to that variation. Most people would probably agree that listening to a radio broadcast of a parliamentary debate is relatively demanding, if we are trying to follow the event closely, while listening to a child reading from a book of fairy stories is much easier. What influences these intuitive assessments? Although a large number of factors are involved, they fall into three principal categories, related to: (1) the type of language we are listening to; (2) our task or purpose in listening, and (3) the context in which listening occurs.

In these terms, the parliamentary debate is difficult under the first and third headings. The language input is hard to follow: the content of what is said may be fairly unpredictable; it may be abstract in nature; it may deal with a range of complex topics, and it will probably be expressed in quite involved linguistic form. There will be a number of different speakers, with different voices and accents. As far as context is concerned, there may be a varying level of background noise; and of course the radio provides us with no visual support for interpreting what is being said or who is speaking. In short, the language input is as demanding as any we might envisage.

But the effect of the complexity of input interacts with our purpose in listening. If we have switched on the radio simply to determine whether the debate has finished or whether today's instalment of our favourite radio serial has started yet, then the listening experience—despite that long list of difficult input features—is not a demanding one. For some listeners, however, the broadcast debate from Westminster will involve a much more difficult task or set of tasks. A business executive, for example, will be paying close attention to what is said in the annual Budget debate because she needs to remember it, either to pass the information on to her colleagues straight away, or to use it at a later stage.

So what makes her task more difficult is her attempt to remember the details of what is said, especially given the type of language in question. As a listener, she is probably consciously going beyond the spoken words and trying to interpret what they imply for her in particular. She is therefore engaging in a great deal of interpretative work, partly because of the language itself, and partly because she has set herself a number of relatively demanding tasks since she wishes to use the information in a variety of ways. In contrast, when a mother listens to a child reading a fairy story, both the language input and the listener's likely purpose combine to make the experience far less difficult.

▶ ## TASK 39

Here are three listening situations:
- a discussion among several speakers about the arguments proposed in the Middle Ages to prove the existence of God
- a tour guide's running commentary as the coach passes the sights of Birmingham
- an elderly man explaining to his grandson who is who in a family photograph.

1 Using your intuitions, arrange the situations in order of difficulty, from the point of view of these different listeners:
- someone who has been asked to summarize the conversations for an absent friend
- someone who has been asked to estimate the length of each conversation.

2 Would your order of difficulty be different if the listeners described above were L2 listeners?

Our two earlier examples, the radio debate and the fairy story, probably represent listening situations close to opposite extremes of a continuum of difficulty, where input and task are hard and easy, respectively. The important thing to remember is that, for all listening situations, the two aspects interact to determine how demanding the experience is for the listener. If we are going to present our students with a series of listening tasks graded for difficulty, then we must have some way of assessing precisely what makes listening more or less difficult, either in terms of the language input or of the listening task. In **4.3** and **4.4** we will be considering the findings of research into the particular listening problems caused by features of input and task.

4.3 Relevant features of listening input

Here we consider what is known about input features that cause a text to be more or less demanding for the listener. Nearly all the relevant research has been conducted with L1 listeners, although we will also be referring to the findings of two studies of L2 listeners' problems with input features. Such L2 research as is available suggests that, at the very least, those features that cause native listeners problems also prove difficult for L2 learners—the point we raised earlier (see Figure 2).

Most research into listening has concerned young native listeners; the number of research studies is relatively small, but it is possible to identify four principal features of language input that have been found to be influential, as far as ease or difficulty of comprehension is concerned. These are: (A) the way in which the *information is organized*; (B) the listeners' *familiarity with the topic*; (C) the *explicitness* of the information given, and (D) the *type* of input.

A Information organization

The most widely investigated feature of information organization is the sequencing of information in simple narrative texts. Where events are described in the order in which they occurred, then the story is better understood and more accurately recalled than if the events are described out of chronological sequence. This has been shown with child and teenage listeners and with adult listeners and readers (Glenn 1978; Bower, Black, and Turner 1979; Stein and Nezworski 1978; Haberlandt and Bingham 1984; Brown, Anderson, Shadbolt, and Lynch 1987). So, for narrative texts, there is at least one well-established criterion by which input can be assessed: the sequence of events. Any disruption or flashback seems to make the information more difficult to understand. Use of this factor in grading listening texts will be illustrated in 7.

▶   TASK 40

The research we have just referred to involved narrative passages. Can you think of examples of *factual* texts in which one sequence of information would be easier for a listener to understand than any other? (One example would be a set of instructions on how to programme a video-cassette player to record.)

In our research we have investigated the relative complexity of the *same informative content* presented in various ways. We found, for example, that listeners were able to remember and pass on more of the content of an expository text (1) when it had an informative title, and (2) when the main points in the text came before illustrations of those points. As we might expect from our earlier discussion of the role of prior knowledge and schemata in listening (**1.4**), the presence of an informative title was the feature that helped listeners most.

Following these findings, it seems likely that, even within a relatively demanding type of language input, information structure can make the text easier or more difficult for the listener. The language teacher could consider the way information is ordered in a factual text when producing or selecting material for her students. She could help the listeners by providing informative titles which help to orientate them to the text they are about to hear. The classroom materials illustrated in 7 include some in which the title is used as a way of grading different narrative inputs and which, in addition, are designed to make the process of knowledge activation a conscious one, through the use of pre-listening tasks.

B Familiarity of topic

Although intuition may suggest that it is easier to listen to a passage on a familiar topic than on an unfamiliar one, there has actually been little research into the role of listeners' knowledge. One of the few studies that has looked at this issue was carried out by Brown, Smiley, Day, Townsend, and Lawton (1977), with seven-year-olds who heard a story about a hunter from the (fictitious) Targa people. A week before being told the story, some of the children had heard a passage that described the Targa as Eskimos living in a cold climate; others had heard that the Targa were American Indians living in the desert.

After listening to the story, all the children were asked questions about climate and living conditions, although the story contained no information about either. Most answers reflected the information the children had acquired a week earlier; but, interestingly, the listeners claimed it *was* in the story they had just been told. This indicates the power of the sources we summarized in Figure 1, since the children (1) were using prior knowledge to interpret what they heard and (2) seemed unaware of the extent to which they were drawing on such knowledge.

Moreover, a third group of children in this study had been presented, in the week before they heard the story, with information about people living in Spain which was irrelevant to the hunting text. Comprehension test results showed that these listeners remembered the story less well than the other two groups, which suggests that a text on a familiar topic is easier to understand, even if the information it contains is novel. So background or schematic knowledge can be shown to play a powerful role in listening performance. However, it should be remembered that such knowledge may *distort*, rather than support, comprehension if it causes the listener/reader to 'force' the content of a text into an existing schematic script. In other words, inappropriately applied background knowledge can lead to misinterpretation.

The positive potential of prior topic knowledge has been observed in listeners as young as six years old. Hare and Devine (1983) found that the amount of prior knowledge of the topic of a story—in their study it was about dolls—was a significant predictor of how much content the listener would recall. So it seems that one kind of easy listening input is one whose topic we already have some knowledge of.

However, Hare and Devine also found that, in contrast to familiarity with the topic, the children's *level of interest* in the doll story had no effect on how much they remembered. One implication of this is that it might be wisest for the teacher to select (or produce) inputs on familiar topics, at least in the early stages of a course. While aiming to choose material that is also of interest to students, she must bear in mind that a high degree of listener interest in a topic will not necessarily lead to more successful listening performance.

▶ TASK 41

You are teaching English oral skills to an intermediate-level group of Italian teenagers, who are preparing for their first visit to Britain. Below are some texts you have available as listening material:

- a live five-minute talk by one of your colleagues on the cities of Italy
- a five-minute conversation between two English teenagers on current fashions in London
- a talk by the trip organizer about the travel arrangements, using the information pack that the students have had for a week or so
- an audiotaped explanation of the workings of the British parliamentary system.

Think about these questions:

1 Which texts would you choose?

2 In which order?

3 What are the factors that influence your decisions?

C Explicitness of information

The third area of research which is relevant to the grading of listening inputs is the amount of information available to the listener, in the sense of the *explicitness* of the text, rather than the physical quantity of information. Three sorts of explicitness have been found to influence ease of comprehension: (1) whether the text contains not only the necessary information but redundant facts as well; (2) whether the speaker provides all the necessary information but no more, and (3) whether the hearer is required to recognize alternative expressions referring to the same character. A variety of research findings (outlined below) suggest that there is often an interaction between these features of the language input and features of the listener, which determines how difficult a particular individual finds a listening task.

1 **Redundancy.** The effects of redundancy have been illustrated by research within the referential communication paradigm (see **2.3**), where listeners have to select one target item from a set, on the basis of a cue from the speaker. Cues can be either *contrastive*, when a single distinguishing feature is mentioned, or *redundant*, where two distinguishing features occur. In one such study, older and younger L1 children (five and nine years old) were found to perform differently (Sonnenschein 1982).

► TASK 42

1 How do you expect the performances of five-year-old and nine-year-old children to differ? Why?

2 Which type of message do you predict would be more difficult— that including redundant information, or that without? Why?

The younger listeners—with less developed memory and listening skills— were not helped by the extra information in the redundant messages, because there was simply too much information for them to process. The older, more proficient listeners were able to exploit the additional support available in the redundant messages, especially in more difficult tasks.

Similar findings have been reported for L2 learners exposed to different kinds of simplified messages by their teachers. Simplifications involving the substitution of a single, more familiar word for an unknown one seem to help all listeners. However, extended redundant paraphrasing of an unknown word (e.g. '. . . the beaver is known as a very industrious *and busy*, uhm, *hard-working* animal') appears to help only more advanced L2 learners. Lower-proficiency students do not benefit and may well be more confused by such 'simplification' (Chaudron 1983a). In other words, as in the findings of the L1 study by Sonnenschein, it seems that the L2 listener has to reach a certain minimum level of proficiency before he can take advantage of the redundancy that a well-meaning native speaker may build into spoken messages.

This could be of considerable relevance in grading listening materials for L2 learners: short, simple messages with the minimum amount of necessary information could be easier for lower-level listeners to use, because they make less demand on the learner in terms of information processing. Learners at more advanced L2 levels may benefit from messages being expanded, paraphrased, etc., because they then have more opportunities to grasp the important details which they have to use in whatever task they are performing.

► TASK 43

Below are two further extracts from the study that was used in Task 32. This time they are taken from the middle of a story about a hat seller whose hats are stolen by monkeys. The same narrator is telling the story to different listeners.

To L1 listener
'eventually the old man woke up + horrified to find that + a lot of his hats had disappeared'

To elementary L2 listener
'eventually the old man woke up + looked at his baskets + and

found everything in a mess + there were hats + all over the place + baskets tipped up + and + a number of them missing'

In the light of Chaudron's research, do you think that the redundant information in the L2 version helped or hindered the learner's comprehension? Which elements would have helped or hindered?

2 Sufficiency of information. Texts containing all the relevant information and no more—and therefore requiring no inference on the part of the listener—are more easily processed by young L1 listeners than those in which they have to do interpretative work of their own. When presented with single sentences, very young children (six years old) have been found to remember only the stated information in the text; on the other hand, older children also recalled implied information. Similarly, in the case of very short stories, the youngest do not always make even 'obvious' connections between sentences (Paris and Lindauer 1976; Small and Butterworth 1981).

So, for young listeners at least, one way in which an input may be easy or difficult is the amount of inferential work the listener is required to do. Explicitly stating all the important relationships in a text probably makes things easier for them. Older foreign learners obviously use the ability to draw inferences when listening in their own language, but may well find that the demands of L2 listening—in the early stages—throw them back on less mature processing habits. So it would seem to be advisable to use explicit material in the earliest stages of an L2 course.

However, care needs to be taken that the provision of explicit information is not perceived by the adult L2 learner as simplification of intellectual *content* rather than of linguistic *form*. Lynch (1988b) reports the results of a small-scale study with adult L2 learners that suggested that a well-meaning native speaker who produces an excessive degree of clarification runs the risk of appearing to be 'talking down' to their L2 audience.

▶ TASK 44

The three listeners to whom these narrative excerpts were told were a native English speaker and two L2 learners at advanced and intermediate levels of English. Can you identify which listener heard which version?

Extract A
'and he takes off his hat and scratches his head + in confusion'

Extract B
'well the man doesn't know what to do + he's very puzzled + and so he scratches his head which means "I don't know what to do"'

Extract C
'this was rather puzzling + so he takes off his hat and scratches his head'
(*Lynch 1987: 7*)

Do you think that either of the L2 learners might have felt that they were being talked down to? If so, why?

In 7 and 8, we will describe classroom materials that provide practice in deciding where inferences can appropriately be made about the implied relationships in a text. The materials always offer the listeners the option of having further information supplied; they themselves decide whether they are confident about making assumptions, or when they wish the texts to be made more fully explicit. This approach allows the explicitness of the language input to be varied flexibly, in response to the listeners' own views about the information they feel they need to complete a particular task. As we shall explain in detail later, we believe this approach is one useful way of grading materials for difficulty in terms of the information supplied in the text.

3 Referring expressions. Another aspect of text explicitness is the way a speaker chooses to refer to the people or objects he mentions, and the effect of these choices on the listener's ease of comprehension. Studies with young L1 listeners have shown that pronouns can cause problems in this respect. Five-year-old listeners experienced difficulties with short texts containing pronominal references, but understood the texts better when the full noun-phrase description of a character was repeated. Older children and adults found pronouns and repeated noun phrases equally easy to understand (Tyler 1983).

In our own research we have found that some teenage L1 listeners have problems with short texts containing a variety of different expressions to refer to the same person or thing. Such variety of expression is common in real-life texts but clearly causes difficulty for quite a number of L1 listeners, even into adolescence. Again, L2 research suggests parallel problems for adult foreign learners. Listeners at lower levels of proficiency seem to find that a simple repetition of a noun phrase is the easiest to comprehend; more advanced learners can cope with both pronouns and varied noun descriptions (Chaudron 1983b).

These studies indicate that texts containing a varied range of referring expressions are potentially problematic, even for relatively mature native listeners. This implies that such texts are difficult and should therefore be tackled after more straightforward texts. But if we wish to offer L1 and L2 listeners real or realistic material, then we have to offer help with this sort of problem. Some of the materials described in 7 are targeted on this area of listening.

▶ TASK 45

Your group of Italian teenagers from Task 41 are now in Britain. You want to make an announcement (in English) about Westminster Abbey. Which of these two versions would be easier for them to understand, and why?

Version A
'Now next we're going to see the most famous church in Britain, the place where all the kings and queens have been crowned, Westminster Abbey. We'll have about half an hour or so to look round this lovely old building. If you get lost, we'll all meet at the west door at four o'clock. Remember it's also a holy place, so behave yourselves.'

Version B
'Now next we're going to see Westminster Abbey. Westminster Abbey is where all the kings and queens have been crowned. We'll have about half an hour to look round the Abbey. If you get lost, we'll meet at the west door of the Abbey at four o'clock. Remember, it *is* an Abbey, so behave yourselves.'

Are there any disadvantages in choosing the 'easy' version?

D Type of input
As we said in **2.3**, most L1 research into listening to different sorts of language input has involved quite young listeners. But there is now a growing amount of evidence that the type of input affects the degree of comprehension difficulty experienced by older listeners, too. From experimental research with teenagers, Brown and Yule (1983a) have categorized spoken texts into three broad types: *static*, *dynamic*, and *abstract*. The terms refer to the differences in the potential complexity of relationships between the things, people, events, and ideas referred to by a speaker.

In a *static* text, such as one describing an object or giving someone instructions on how to assemble a model, the relationship between items is likely to be fixed. However, telling a story or recounting an incident demands *dynamic* use of language. It will probably involve shifts of scene and time; the people or characters in the text may drift in and out of the story, or their relationship to each other may change—for example, a married couple may get divorced. Finally, *abstract* texts are those where the focus is on someone's ideas and beliefs, rather than concrete objects; for instance, they might be saying why they chose a particular school or university.

▶ TASK 46

Here is a list of various situations in which you might need to refer to a compact disc player. In each case, decide whether you think the language would fall into the static, dynamic, or abstract category. You may decide they will have elements of more than one type.

1 Telling the shop assistant which of the four compact disc player models you want to buy. They are displayed on shelves behind him.

2 Telling a friend how the sound quality of compact discs compares with that of an LP record.

3 Telling the manageress of the shop where you bought the player the week before that you now realize the shop assistant overcharged you. You have lost your receipt.

Brown and Yule have summarized the implications of experimental findings in what they term 'a fairly informal grid', shown in Figure 3.

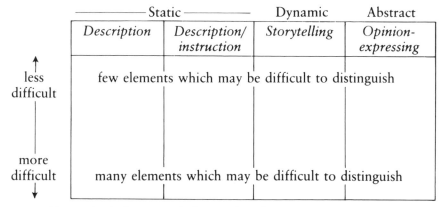

Figure 3: A framework for grading listening input

(*Adapted from Brown and Yule 1983a: 107*)

There are two scales of difficulty built into the grid. First, difficulty increases from left to right, *between types of input*. This corresponds to the static/dynamic/abstract relationship. So description is assumed to represent the simplest sort of language input and opinion-expressing the most difficult. Second, there is the top-to-bottom scale of relative complexity, *within any one type of input*. Here, Brown and Yule suggest that one of the factors that can make one language text more complex than another is the number of important and potentialy confusable elements it contains. For example, telling or listening to a story with two male characters will be rather more difficult than a similar story with one character of each sex.

► TASK 47

1 Think about that last sentence. Why should the first story present more problems than the second?

2 Apart from the number of characters it contains, what other elements of a story might be adjusted to create more or fewer problems for the teller/listener?

Notice that we have just been talking about both sides of the storytelling process—speaking and listening. In fact Brown and Yule's grid is based on experimental work focusing on oral *production* and so their framework represents the relative scale of difficulty experienced by speakers, rather than listeners (for details, see Brown *et al.* 1984).

However, similar results have been reported for the receptive skills, in both listening and reading. In an investigation of L1 listening skills, involving the same age-group as the speakers in the 1984 study (Brown *et al.* 1987), the listeners experienced a similar increase in difficulty between and within types of input, that is, both horizontally and vertically as shown in Figure 3. In the case of reading comprehension, adult L1 readers have been shown to find narrative materials easier to understand than expository texts (Graesser *et al.* 1980; Kintsch and Young 1984). So there seem to be reasonable grounds for using the informal grid of difficulty as a basis for the grading of listening complexity.

It is important to bear in mind, though, that the 'vertical' factor of complexity highlighted in Brown and Yule's grid—the *number of elements* in a text that need to be distinguished—is only one aspect of its likely difficulty. Above we have discussed various other aspects of a language text that can affect its ease of comprehension: the way the information is organized, its explicitness, the familiarity of the topic, and so on. These are among the grading factors that will be discussed in relation to the teaching materials illustrated in Section Two.

4.4 Relevant factors in listening tasks and contexts

We have considered how the nature of the input can cause the listener more difficulty or less. Now we want to examine the impact of the other major aspects of listening, the task and the context. As we stressed in **2.6**, the overall difficulty confronting a listener is a combination of these three dimensions of listening.

Processing load
Two important factors of difficulty are the amount of information that has to be processed and the amount of time available. It would be more difficult to respond to the instruction 'Give me the brass screw', if there were lots of screws of varying sizes and materials in view, or if you were under time pressure. Even when the *message* itself is perfectly adequate and perfectly understood, the task can make a successful performance more or less easy to achieve.

This has been shown in an experimental listening task with young native listeners (Sonnenschein 1982). Even adult L1 listeners can be helped if the information processing demands of the task are reduced. For example, if you hear the relevant message 'Give me the brass screw' *before* you are presented with a collection of objects, you know precisely what to focus your attention on. On the other hand, if you have to study a work-bench full of objects and *then* listen to the instructions, you will naturally wonder what you are going to be asked to do; in this way, the listening task is made more difficult. Again, the effect of sequence has been shown in an experiment with a wide range of L1 listeners (Sonnenschein and Whitehurst 1982). For our purposes, it is interesting that having the message presented immediately before seeing the collection of objects was most helpful for the youngest, least able listeners.

▶ **TASK 48**

Imagine that the text below is a spoken message. Read it through, then cover it up and answer the questions that follow.

'Well, there are lots of flights from Glasgow Airport. During the summer you can fly to all the main holiday destinations—you know, Spain, Majorca, Minorca, Portugal, Rhodes, Corfu, Crete, Yugo-slavia. There are also the scheduled European flights. That's Amsterdam, Paris, Munich. They fly all year, twice a week I think: Monday and Thursday for Amsterdam, Tuesday and Friday Paris, and Wednesday and Friday Munich. You can always get the shuttle to London every hour, so that means you can fly almost anywhere. The holiday flights are limited to the high season, so if it's October you might well have to go via Heathrow.'

1 Cover the text. Does it represent an easy or difficult task for a listener having to answer one of these alternative questions?
– Can you fly direct to Munich from Glasgow on a Thursday?
– Are there many summer flights from Glasgow?
2 How could the tasks be made easier?

The L1 research we have referred to highlights the problems that confront listeners when they are presented with (aural or visual) information without being sure what they will be asked to do with it. Under such circumstances, they cannot determine which input features are relevant and should be attended to, and which irrelevant features can be ignored.

This implies that if—as is often the case in the language classroom—listeners are presented with relatively long and informationally dense messages, before being asked questions on the content, then they are being subjected to an extremely demanding type of listening task. The experimental results also suggest that, if the listeners are specifically told in advance which features of the ensuing message are relevant to their listening purpose, the task is likely to be considerably easier. Given this sort of support, the listener can attend selectively to the appropriate parts of the message and therefore decrease the amount of information processing and memorization involved.

So the task is facilitated if the teacher provides adequate pre-listening orientation activities, particularly in the early part of any course, in order to make clear the listening purpose and the specific task details. Some classroom materials are designed to do this, and also to reduce the information processing load on listeners, through tasks that are completed as the learners listen. Having to make a number of responses during a task, each one immediately following a short segment of input, means that memory load is kept to a minimum.

Visual support
Listeners benefit from further help in the form of visual support material that is designed to assist their interpretation of what they hear. Experimental evidence of the value of this feature of listening tasks comes in an L1 study by Pratt, Bates, and Wickers (1980), who compared children's ability to evaluate the adequacy of a message they had heard, either from memory or using a picture as a memory aid. Listeners given the visual support did better. Mueller (1980) reported similar results with L2 learners, using a very simple line drawing as an aid to the comprehension of an audiotaped interview. The amount and type of visual support can be graded, as will be discussed further in 6 and 7.

We should, in passing, mention one form of visual support that has recently become available to language teachers, though as yet to a relatively small minority—videocassette materials. Throughout this Section we have emphasized the fact that listening is not simply an aural activity and that successful comprehension involves the exploitation of all possible sources of useful information. Since the medium of videotape provides access to more information than is the case with audiotape, it should follow that—at least for some types of comprehension activity—video material will offer the language learner greater support.

▶ TASK 49

What additional types of information does video material make available to the language learner? (It may be helpful to refer again to Figure 1).

What are the advantages of using video material for the practice and development of listening skills?

However, the very richness of the data that the television screen makes available to the learner is also a potential source of confusion and distraction. As MacWilliam (1986) points out, despite the reasonable claims that video material adds motivation and interest, there has so far been very little research into which aspects of comprehension are more effectively practised using videotapes. We cannot go into this issue in any detail in this book, but offer suggestions under 'Further Reading'. As far as our central point is concerned, it seems likely that the wealth of information the video provides makes the element of control, achieved by means of a principled approach to grading complexity, that much more necessary.

Group format

One aspect of the classroom listening context that is independent of the language input is the decision whether to adopt a format of group or individual work. The same message can be played either to individual listeners, or to groups for discussion. The latter method is attractive for a number of reasons.

▶ ## TASK 50

Language teachers seem to agree that there are advantages to group work, where it is a practical possibility. What advantages—or drawbacks—would you say there might be in using group work for listening activities?

We might wish to use group-based work for general pedagogic reasons, such as a belief in the importance of increasing cooperation and cohesiveness among students. Then there are more specifically language-learning oriented arguments: classroom researchers such as Pica and Doughty (1985) have offered evidence for the positive role of group work in promoting a linguistic environment likely to assist L2 learning. (The issue of alternative classroom groupings is discussed in detail in Wright: *Roles of Teachers and Learners*, also published in this Scheme.)

Recent L1 research using controlled comparisons of the performances of groups and individuals has confirmed the benefits of group work. Anderson and Boyle (in progress) have found that groups of fourteen- and fifteen-year-olds performed listening tasks significantly more effectively than individuals. When group work was combined with pre-listening activities designed to activate listeners' knowledge of the topic it also led to better recall of the task, and to better subsequent performances when the group members listened individually. Similar results have been reported for primary age children (Yager, Johnson, and Johnson 1985).

Type of task

The factors we have considered so far—ways of minimizing the information processing load, the provision of visual support, and group work—could be thought of as aspects of the listening *context*. The other factor that needs to be borne in mind, if we wish to create a graded programme of work, is the nature of the listening *task* itself. Different tasks present the listener with varying degrees of complexity. For example, as we saw in 2.5, teenage L1 listeners find that producing a summary of a message is more problematic than recalling the complete content, even when the message is the same.

▶ TASK 51

> If producing summaries of listening texts appears to be a compara-
> tively difficult task for L1 listeners, it is likely to be at least as difficult
> for L2 listeners. What do you think might be the additional
> (speaking or listening) problems involved in the case of summarizing
> L2 listening material?

Summarizing a message may be difficult because, like distinguishing fact
from opinion, it is an *evaluative* listening task. The listener has to evaluate
which items of information are important and should be included in the
summary, and which are less essential and can be omitted.

Another evaluative listening task that has been shown to cause difficulty
even among L1 listeners is distinguishing factual argument from unsup-
ported opinion. In the study referred to in **2.6**, Neville (1985) played
eleven- and thirteen-year-old native listeners a taped conversation between
parents discussing whether or not to buy a pet. One parent presented facts,
the other opinions. After hearing the tape, the children were asked to say
which parent had given the more reasoned argument and why. This task
proved to be even more difficult for them than an earlier summary task.

So tasks that involve an immediate response (e.g. drawing or ordering
pictures) are found to be easier than those that require a process of listening
and then selecting (e.g. summary). These in turn are perceived as less
difficult than ones in which fact and opinion have to be distinguished. It
would therefore seem sensible for the language teacher to delay these more
difficult tasks until her students have demonstrated substantial competence
on the simpler task types. We will be illustrating the use of the task as a
grading factor in **6** and **7**.

4.5 Summary

Listening is an essential skill for successful communication. Effective
listeners utilize a wide range of information sources simultaneously. Even
in native users of a language, listening skills are not always fully developed;
the skills involved in the cognitive or information-transfer aspects of
listening cause the greatest problems.

Even native listeners can benefit from training with appropriate listening
texts and tasks. On these grounds we would argue that it is important to
provide foreign learners of a language with training specifically directed at
listening skills. To do this effectively requires a graded programme of
listening work.

In grading a listening exercise we have to bear in mind the three principal
aspects of listening: (1) the type of input; (2) the support provided by the
listening context, and (3) the kind of task involved. In Sections Two and
Three we outline various approaches to these design problems, including
those available in the form of published materials, and also our own work
with L1 and L2 learners.

Demonstration
Listening materials

5 Listening in the L2 classroom

5.1 Introduction

In Section One we discussed what is involved in the processes of real-life listening with the aim of isolating the likely features of comprehension difficulty that would need to be taken into consideration in designing programmes to develop students' listening comprehension. In this section we move to issues of direct practical concern to L2 teachers: the form and content of listening activities in the classroom.

In 5 we consider what notions of L2 listening the writers of published courses appear to subscribe to and we set out some of the principal implications of the research reviewed in Section One. In 6 we will be looking at extracts from a variety of listening comprehension courses and analysing the extent to which those materials display a principled foundation, of the sort we have argued for. In 7 we illustrate materials intended to develop learners' listening skills in a graded programme and use them as the basis for evaluating the classroom activity of listening. This leads readers on to the exploration of their own classrooms in Section Three.

5.2 What counts as 'listening'?

What do teachers actually mean when they talk about 'listening' as a classroom activity? The answer is likely to vary with the specific teaching context. For some teachers, 'listening' would be a complete timetabled session by that name, using published material specifically designed to practise the aural comprehension skill; we might call this *autonomous* listening material. For others, it might be only part of a lesson based on a global language course book that includes the exploitation of recorded materials that are linked—structurally, functionally, thematically—with the current learning focus. We could call this *ancillary* listening material.

Many teachers would assume that 'listening' has to involve the use of tapes and electronic equipment. They may express regret that they 'cannot do listening' because their school or institution does not provide (or cannot afford) audio- or videocassette recorders, radio, television, and so on. However, if we take the teaching/learning world as a whole, the majority of language teachers do not have access to aids such as these.

For reasons of space, we will be concentrating in 5 or 6 on autonomous listening materials, and illustrating various points by drawing on published courses. But this should not be taken to imply that teachers are totally dependent on what is available on the commercial market. Indeed, in 7 we will be presenting examples of the sort of listening programme that teachers might be able to create for themselves, even if they do not have access to published print and cassette materials.

Clearly, our assumptions about what 'listening' can or should involve are influenced by our individual circumstances. It is inevitable that 'listening' means different things to different people. The important question is: 'Do we know whether one way of practising listening is better than any other?'

▶ TASK 52

Here is a list of six activities that might engage your students' listening skills. Assume, for the purpose of this task, that the language used in each case is the target language.

- You play the students an off-air recording of a radio programme.
- The students work in pairs and tell each other about incidents from their own lives.
- The students follow your classroom instructions (for example, as you get them to rearrange furniture for group work).
- You play the cassette that accompanies the main language coursebook the class is using.
- You clarify a language point that has caused the students difficulty.
- The students listen as you read a story aloud.

1 Are you able to rearrange these activities in order of priority from 'most useful' to 'least useful' as listening practice, from the language learner's point of view?
2 If so, what criteria did you use?

In our current state of knowledge of language learning, it would be foolish to claim that any one of the variations of listening in Task 52 offers a quicker or more effective route to success than the others. All listening *probably* helps; as teachers we may have personal opinions as to which listening activities help learners more—but at this stage it is still a matter of opinions rather than certainties.

The role assigned by language course writers and teachers to listening as a learner activity is closely related to their overall view of how classroom L2 learning/teaching works best. Benson and Hjelt (1978) suggest there are three main historical views of the role of listening in the whole L2 learning process.

Firstly, there is the view that language learning is a *linear process*. Learners should start with the spoken medium skills (listening and speaking) and move later to those of the written medium (reading and writing). Listening is the means to immediate oral production, which is the imitation of spoken forms.

The second view is of language learning as an *integrative process*. All four conventional skills should be introduced simultaneously, so that practice in one can support and reinforce practice in the others. Characteristic of this approach is the view that 'early listening comprehension materials should be kept within the limits of structural patterns being learned' (Rivers 1971: 130).

Supporters of the third view believe that language learning is best thought of as a *comprehension-focused process*. Emphasizing the parallels with L1 acquisition and informal (non-classroom) L2 learning, some authors see listening as the key to successful learning, or at least as the primary source of language experience (as we saw in **3.2**). They think that the texts that teachers use to provide comprehensible input should include items at a linguistic level one stage ahead of the learners' current level of L2 production, so that comprehension can, so to speak, 'drive' learning.

► TASK 53

Here are three statements about the teaching of L2 listening to beginners. They translate the three historical views into a form that teachers might use in discussion with colleagues.

Statement A
Listening needs to be combined with speaking, to allow beginners to relate the sounds on tape with those they make themselves and to give them confidence in speaking the language. Reading and writing should come later.

Statement B
Learners need to develop listening, speaking, reading, and writing in parallel, right from the very start. By getting beginners to participate in simple activities in all four skills you can give them a more rounded picture of how the L2 is used. It is easier for them to learn the language when they can make their own connections between one skill and the others.

Statement C
What initial learners need is confidence from success in understanding the spoken language, not in producing it. So the first lessons of any L2 course should concentrate solely on listening. The learners ought to be allowed to answer questions in their L1 to develop the necessary self-assurance.

Which of those three statements comes closest to expressing your own attitudes to the place of listening in an L2 beginners' course? Would you want to make any alterations or qualifications?

The theoretical issues raised in Tasks 52 and 53 affect classroom teaching in concrete and practical ways. Firstly, they influence the way we see the function of listening in the classroom. Secondly, they have consequences for the type of materials that we use in the classroom—or, at least, they should. In practice, it may well be that we select particular materials for other shorter-term reasons, rather than on the basis of global and systematic principles. It is very easy to allow classroom constraints to dominate our teaching choices at the expense of longer-term criteria.

▶ ## TASK 54

A recent survey (White 1987) of the preferences for particular published listening materials among EFL teachers working in Britain, Europe, and Japan suggests that the following are among the reasons for teachers' satisfaction with particular listening materials:

'good for starting discussions'
'can be used for self-access learning'
'contains a variety of tasks'
'entertaining'
'easy to use'
'practises guessing from context'
'amusing'
'uses authentic material'
'consolidates language'

Some of those reasons would apply equally well to materials practising the other language skills, such as reading. Are there any that are *specifically* related to the skill of listening?

We are not suggesting that factors such as the students' likely interest in a particular topic, or how easy a particular set of materials is for the teacher to use, should be excluded from consideration of what to do in the classroom. But there is some risk that, in coming to decisions about which materials to use, we will be motivated only by factors such as student interest; we might easily lose sight of the grading principles that should underlie an L2 classroom course that includes listening. We will be taking up this issue in 6 and 7.

5.3 Teaching listening or testing listening?

So far we have talked about *teaching* or *developing* listening. We need now to confront a problematic and basic issue: how is the *teaching* of listening different from the *testing* of listening? The difficulty is that the classroom methods that most teachers think of as tools for teaching listening comprehension in fact amount to a form of continuous testing: 'It is a truism to point out that the technique of asking questions after a reading or listening task is a testing technique and not a teaching technique' (McDonough 1981: 74).

Although it may be a truism, the distinction that McDonough draws our attention to is still often blurred in listening materials. However, Mary Underwood—probably the best-known author of British EFL listening courses—has been influential in trying to change teachers' views on the relative balance between testing and teaching. Her listening courses (e.g. Underwood 1971, 1976, 1979; Underwood and Barr 1980) themselves reflect a general change over time in relation to the testing/teaching issue and others, and we will be illustrating that development in various tasks in 5 and 6.

In the introduction to one of her more recent courses, Underwood makes this comment for teachers about to use her material:

> It is important that the exercises should *not* be treated as *test items*. They are designed as aids to aural comprehension practice, directing the students' attention to 'focal points' on the tape so that they will learn to listen more effectively.
> (*Underwood 1979: 4*)

The point that she is stressing here is that teachers should stop thinking of comprehension questions primarily as a means of *assessing* how much learners have understood and should use listening exercises as a framework for *assisting* them to understand spoken language. In Task 55 we consider how this works in practice.

▶ TASK 55

Below are extracts from the first two units of Underwood's (1979) course. They share the theme 'People talking about the things they like'. Analyse what Underwood's exercises require the learner to do, then consider the three questions that follow the extracts.

Unit 1.1: Felix talks about his job as a schoolmaster

 Exercise 1

Listen carefully to what Felix says and decide which of the following statements is true and which is false.

1. It took Felix a very long time to choose a job.
2. Felix believes he chose the right job.
3. The system Felix works in is very structured, with each person being someone else's boss.
4. Each group of boys is taught by only one teacher.
5. Felix says his job is like working in an office.
6. Felix would like a different job.
7. Felix has to do the same things every day.
8. Felix teaches boys of different ages.

(*Underwood 1979: 10*)

Unit 1.2: Matthew talks about mountain holidays

  Exercise 1

Having heard the tape, try to answer each of the following questions briefly. You may need to listen again to find the answers.

1   Does Matthew like all mountains?
2   What does he think the Swiss Alps are good for?
3   What, in his view, are the Swiss Alps not good for?
4   Does Matthew think the Pyrenees are good for walking?
5   How long does it take to go up and down a Welsh mountain?
6   What would Matthew find embarrassing?

(*Underwood 1979: 11*)

1 In what way are the instructions for the two exercises different? Is one task more demanding as a result?

2 In what way would the author's questions help the learners 'to listen more effectively' to each text?

3 In what way do you think that listening to Felix discussing his work would help the students 'to listen more effectively' to Matthew talking about the Swiss Alps?

The third of our questions could be paraphrased as 'How does listening to one piece of language help learners to cope with others?' The usual answer runs like this: 'The basic problem that foreign listeners have is that they are not used to everyday language being spoken naturally. So they need practice in getting used to such speech. The more practice they get, the more skilled they will become.' The argument is that listeners lack exposure to the language and the listening course provides that exposure.

However, the studies we discussed in Section One strongly suggest that simply providing exposure to spoken language texts and *testing* learners' comprehension, as many listening courses do, is less effective than adopting a *teaching* approach. A teaching approach would involve not only providing helpful support exercises but also grading the learners' experience of complexity. That makes it necessary to analyse what the potential sources of difficulty are and to provide graded practice in dealing with them.

▶ **TASK 56**

We can illustrate the difference between a teaching exercise and a testing exercise by contrasting the approach adopted in two more listening courses by Underwood. We have chosen to compare these particular exercises for two reasons. Firstly, they appeared in different decades and illustrate the shift in the approach to the teaching of listening that we mentioned earlier. Secondly, they are directly comparable since they are both based on recordings of librarians explaining their work.

Exercise A

> I *Now that you have listened to the whole conversation, look at the questions below. Listen carefully again and answer the questions by choosing the right answer from A B C or D.*
> 1. With general tickets, borrowers can take . . . . . from the library.
> A fiction only   C both fiction and non-fiction
> B non-fiction only   D none of these

(*Underwood 1971: 4*)

Exercise B

> Liz is a librarian in an academic library. She does a number of different tasks every day. List five things she might be expected to do. Then, while you are listening to Extract H, tick any jobs she mentions which are on your list.

(*Underwood and Barr 1980: 12*)

1 Compare what the listeners are being asked to do—and in which order—in the two exercises. Which of the two do you think is more oriented towards teaching (i.e. helping the learners perform the task)?

2 What is the source of the help they get? (If necessary, look back to Figure 1 in **1.4**.)

One of the differences between the exercises is that Exercise A leads the learners only to the answer of that particular question. Exercise B, on the other hand, encourages the students to adopt an appropriate strategy. The simple instruction 'List five things . . .' requires the application of what the listeners already *know*, to help them understand what they are about to *hear*.

5.4 Listening or remembering?

As we saw in **1.3**, the fact that you cannot remember something does not necessarily mean that you did not understand it at the time you heard it. So one of the criticisms made of the conventional method of presentation of comprehension material—questions asked after the listening activity—is that students' incorrect answers may be caused by their being unable to recall the precise details of what they heard—and actually understood at the time of hearing. Indeed, L1 listeners tend to 'translate' what they have understood from the form of words that the speaker used into a form that preserves meaning but not surface detail.

Apart from the issue of the form (original wording, or reasonable equivalent) in which we remember points in what we have heard, there is the question of the amount of detail we need to recall, having understood the speaker's point. Under normal conditions in conversational contexts we would not feel we had failed as listeners if we were unable to repeat our interlocutor's utterances word for word. But what do we expect of L2 listeners?

▶ TASK 57

This listening exercise is from O'Neill and Scott (1974), Unit 13. The students hear segments from an interview with Mr Thurlow, an expert on automation.

These are the questions at the end of the first part of the interview:

---

1 On this particular assembly line, what do the girls do?
2 What does the first girl do?
3 Mr Thurlow mentions another girl. What does she do?
4 What 'mechanism' is Mr Thurlow talking about?
5 How difficult is the operation?
6 How many times in a day would a girl do the same thing on the machine?

(*O'Neill and Scott 1974: 85*)

Without access to the recording or transcript, what is your impression of the degree of detail the student is asked to recall in order to achieve correct answers?

In their concern to find material for comprehension questions, course writers can exaggerate the amount of information that a fully competent L1 listener would find it necessary to recall under real-life conditions. As a result, the 'world' created by listening course writers is distorted: like a hall of mirrors that magnify one particular aspect of the person standing in front of them, comprehension questions may encourage L2 listeners (and teachers) to attach excessive importance to attempting to understand specific bits of information.

▶ TASK 58

Look back to question 6 in Task 57. Then read the extract below, which comes from the relevant part of the interview transcript.

INTERVIEWER:	How many times in a day would a girl do this particular operation?
MR THURLOW:	Oh, twelve, fourteen thousand.
INTERVIEWER:	Fourteen thousand times?
MR THURLOW:	Yes,//
INTERVIEWER:	Yes.//
MR THURLOW:	Sometimes, yes.

(*O'Neill and Scott 1974: 174*)

What answer to question 6 do you think would be given by:
– Mr Thurlow?
– the course writers?

So there is the problem of memory: under normal circumstances we do not rely on precise word-for-word recall. Approximate answers are often adequate in real life, but the post-text comprehension question leads learners to expect speakers to deliver tidy packages of information, rather than the rough-and-ready chunks that are typical in conversation. As we can see in the example in Task 58, the meaning of a piece of spoken language—even containing something as apparently clear-cut as a number—may in fact be more blurred than the 'official' answer to the course writers' question allows.

5.5 Orientation of questions

In Section One we referred to Brown and Yule's division of occasions of language use into primarily transactional or information-oriented events, and primarily interactional or listener-oriented events. Teachers or course writers may choose to direct the learner's attention either to the message or to the interlocutors' relationship.

▶ TASK 59

The questions overleaf come from different units of *Start Listening* (McLean 1981), a course for elementary EFL learners. Is their focus transactional or interactional?

Exercise A

YOUR AIM	Listen to Garry and Eric. What are they talking about? After each BLEEP, write (or draw) your answer.

Exercise B

YOUR AIM	Listen to Alan and Garry. Listen to Garry's answers. Is he feeling impatient? After each BLEEP, say 'Impatient' or 'Not impatient'.

Exercise C

YOUR AIM	Listen to Garry. Sometimes he sneezes (ATCHOO!), and you can't hear a word. What kind of word is missing? After each BLEEP, tick the right box.

EXAMPLE	*Garry:* Hello? Alan? It's Garry here. Can you come and see me? I'm feeling very ATCHOO!!! ● . . .	found	a cold	ill ✓

(*McLean 1981: 41, 15, 42–3*)

This particular course was unusual at the time it appeared, since it included practice in recognizing—at this elementary L2 level—things like speakers' attitudes to each other (exercise B), which had previously been regarded as territory reserved for more advanced learners.

In general, though, most listening comprehension courses focus on the information element in recorded material, even when the original event was an informal conversation rather than a transactional exchange of facts. In this way they may create the impression that such events arise in response to a speaker's need to give the listener information, rather than arising as part of their social relationship.

▶ **TASK 60**

Here is the final section of a conversational anecdote about the death of a balloonist, used in an intermediate-level listening course (Underwood 1976). This is printed only in the teacher's book. Consider these points:

– What is the reaction of the original (native) listener, Alan?
– How much detail do we *know* he has understood?

> GERRY   ... He was dead
> when we found him so, you know, there was no chance of
> really finding out what had happened. But the
> extraordinary thing about this, is, his widow insisted on
> carrying on the family tradition of balloon-mastering, and
> she has since then filled and inflated my balloon and I've
> flown. But he was a very, very great balloon-master, you
> know, and it is incredible to think that a man got away
> with this once and then less than a week later he met his
> death ... in this way. Another quite extraordinary thing, of
> course, is the balloon came down and landed quite safely
> twenty-five miles away.
> ALAN What a tragic story!
> GERRY It *was* really because he was a very great man and
> very, very well known in ballooning circles.

(*Underwood 1976: 177–8*)

Now look at the final two questions that the L2 listeners have to
answer.

> 9 Jaeger's wife
>   A Insisted on flying the balloon that killed her
>   husband
>   B went on ballooning, in the family tradition
>   C gave up all contacts with ballooning
>   D said she'd never balloon again, but did
>
> 10 It is almost impossible to believe, according to Gerry,
>   that Jaeger
>   A should have been a balloon-master
>   B should be dead when they found him
>   C should have had the same sort of mishap twice
>   and should have been all right the first time but
>   killed the second time
>   D should have tried again after nearly having the
>   same accident the week before

(*Underwood 1976: 81*)

3 How is the level of detail of the response demanded of the learners
   different from that of the original listener?

One effect of comprehension questions such as these may be to alter the
response of the listener from that originally intended. Rather than listening
for the overall outcome (happy or unhappy, successful or unsuccessful) of a

social anecdote, learners have to cope with potentially confusing detail—and of the sort that the native listener might in any case discard, ignore, or forget. As eavesdroppers to the Task 62 recording we cannot be certain, from Alan's reaction, that he has actually understood more than something as general as 'the man died'.

Naturally, as classroom teachers, we want to make maximum use of any piece of language material—particularly if we are teaching in difficult conditions and without easy access to L2 material. But if we treat every piece of L2 conversational data as a package of detailed information for the learner to unwrap, we do two things that can distort the listening purpose: (1) we encourage the belief that to understand a text you have to get questions right; (2) we make the listening task more demanding than it was for the original listener.

5.6 Types of response: learner involvement

We have so far talked about the possible difference between the original interactional purpose of a piece of language and the transactional focus provided by the listening exercises written to accompany it. Another way in which the course writer/teacher may alter the nature of the learner/listener's comprehension of a text is through the type of response required in a particular task.

Eavesdropper or participant

Firstly, there is the question of whether we make the learners eavesdroppers or participants. Students listening to L2 material can be put in the position of the original listener, for example by being asked to draw up a list of items that the speaker wants the listener to buy; in this case, the relationship between the speaker and the (secondary) listener in the classroom is similar to that between the speaker and the original listener.

Alternatively, the task may require them to observe and analyse the behaviour of the speaker(s) in the recording: this might require a response with a transactional focus ('Which of the two people was arguing for, and which against, longer prison sentences?') or an interactional focus ('What is your impression of the relationship between Mrs Fortescue and Miss Evans?').

▶ TASK 61

The two exercises below are taken from different units of *Elementary Task Listening* (Stokes 1984). Do they require the listeners to involve themselves in the interaction (by responding like the original listener), or to distance themselves from the speakers (by analysing what is happening)?

15 Making sense of a television interview

What were the two women talking about? Make a list of the important words which helped you reach this conclusion.

30

(Stokes 1984: 30)

── (LISTENING)──

17 Using a multi-storey car park

Indicate the correct order of the instructions by numbering the photographs 1—6.

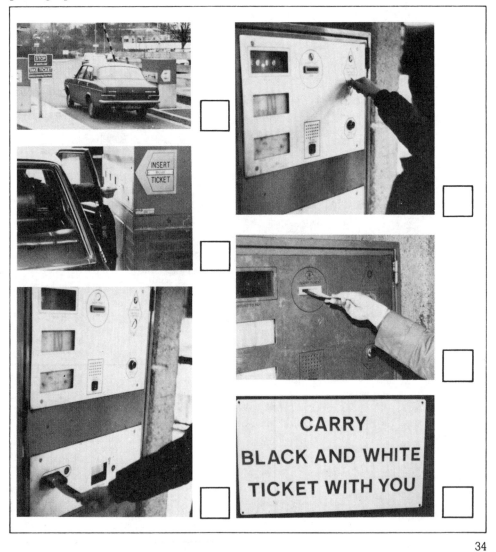

34

(Stokes 1984: 34)

Accessibility versus acceptability

In some comprehension courses, the learner is required to respond to the content of the text in different ways, in a series of tasks. A typical sequence might include the following:

1 The teacher plays a recording of a couple arguing the rights and wrongs of using animals in medical experiments.
2 The learners then work through a set of comprehension activities that concentrate on the factual content of the two speakers' contributions.
3 The learners then discuss their own views on the subject, supporting one or either of the recorded speakers or setting out an alternative position.

In a sequence of this sort, the learners are being encouraged to respond to a language text in two distinct ways. We could summarize these by saying that they are being asked to cope with the *accessibility* and the *acceptability* of the speakers' views (terms from Widdowson 1983). In the second stage of the sequence, they are asked to show what/how much they have understood of the speakers' respective points of view. In other words, they are being required to indicate how *accessible* the text is to them. In the third, the task demand is different: they are being asked to give their own view on the topic, to relate to the text as individuals. Here, they are showing how *acceptable* the content expressed in the language is to them.

To some extent the distinction between accessibility and acceptability is related to that between transactional and interactional types of language. However, even spoken texts that are essentially transactional, for example an academic lecture, can lead listeners to respond in terms of both 'Have I understood?' and 'Do I agree with this?'

▶   TASK 62

The discussion points shown below are taken from a lecture comprehension course (Lynch 1983). By the time the students discuss the six points, they have already worked through three earlier stages: pre-listening discussion; listening/note-taking; comparison of notes.

In this case the listening text is a lecture on the problems of competition for land use between food crops and fuel crops. Read through the six points and consider the two questions that follow.

Stage 4—Post-listening discussion

1 Can you explain these terms from the talk: *fossil fuels, gasohol* and *marginal land*?
2 Do you think that the US corn (maize) alcohol project was a good idea? Why (not)?
3 What would be the advantages for Brazil of using cassava rather than sugar cane for alcohol production?
4 Do you think that Lester Brown's proposal would help to solve the possible competition for land between food crops and fuel crops?
5 The speaker ends her talk by saying: 'If nothing is done, there could be a very serious problem, and this conflict between the use of land for food or for fuel could turn into *something other than an economic problem.*' What do you imagine she means by that?
6 Do you think her fears are justified?

(*Lynch 1983: 72*)

1 Which of the questions are designed to focus the learners' attention on the *accessibility* of what the speaker has said, and which ones deal with its *acceptability*? Can you be sure in all cases?
2 What are the information sources (cf. Figure 1 in **1.4**) that the listeners can draw on in their discussion?

Allowing for the listener's individual response to a piece of language represents a fundamental extension of the classroom activity of 'listening'. It is one way of making classroom listening more like real-life language use. Some people might object that it places unrealistic demands on the L2 listener, since in real life even native speakers do not necessarily have definite own views on *every* topic that they hear others discussing.

On the other hand, if teachers/course writers only require the 'what did Mrs Fortescue say?' type of response, learners are in fact being encouraged to treat L2 texts as something empty of meaning for them as individuals. Since we do naturally react in a vaguely positive or negative fashion to things we hear people say about things, it makes pedagogic sense to incorporate this into listening materials by encouraging an individual response from listeners in the classroom.

5.7 Task materials

One of the striking aspects of recent listening materials is the variety of tasks that course writers now use. Brown has referred to the 'astonishing range of inventions poured into the construction of attractively packaged materials' (Brown 1986a: 4). The available surveys of task types (e.g. Ur 1984) provide the reader with lists of activities; however, they do not offer teachers any guidance in grading or sequencing different tasks.

▶ TASK 63

Here is a selection of task types. Can you arrange them in order 1–8, from most difficult to least difficult?

A listen and follow (e.g. a route on a map)
B listen and enjoy (e.g. a story)
C listen and do (e.g. label, tick, draw)
D listen and react (affectively, i.e. emotionally)
E listen and complete (e.g. a gapped transcript)
F listen and correct (amend errors in a summary)
G listen and discuss (e.g. rights and wrongs)
H listen and recall

Did you encounter any problems in deciding on the order?

In this book we are less concerned with the surface detail of such tasks than with the principles that underlie them. At the same time as praising the attractiveness of materials, Brown warns that excessive concern with 'packaging' may distract attention from the learner's need for a systematically graded programme:

> Most courses on the market still claim to present 'graded' materials, but the authors don't specify what their principles of grading are—and careful study of the sequence of materials usually fails to reveal any principle of grading.
> (*Brown 1986a: 4*)

In 6 we examine the extent to which course writers do (or do not) claim to present a graded series of listening experiences, and the justifiability of their claims. In 7 we illustrate sample materials from a programme designed to offer graded exposure to listening problems and suggest ways of evaluating these and other listening materials.

6 Approaches to grading L2 listening

6.1 Introduction

In this part of the book we consider possible solutions to the grading problem, in the form of both published teaching material and theoretical design proposals. We examine the claims that the authors make about their ability to grade the learners' experience of difficulty in the light of the research evidence discussed in **4**.

Probably very few teachers would disagree with the idea that, in principle, teaching anything necessarily involves deciding (1) what the elements are that make up the knowledge or skill to be taught, and (2) in which order to teach/present those elements. In practice, these two decisions are far from straightforward. Newmark warned that we should not take for granted our ability to grade language teaching material, since it

> assumes that the course programmer can decide intelligently what items to present and in what sequence they should be presented. But in fact there is as yet no such theory of language teaching that would guide those decisions.
> (*Newmark 1981: 47*)

Nevertheless, until recently the writers of listening comprehension materials have generally acted as if there were agreed, fixed guidelines on grading that they could follow.

▶ TASK 64

Which of these definitions of L2 grading seems to you to be the most useful—and why?

'the building-up of a selected system in the best order possible'
(*Mackey 1954: 58*)

'a progression from simple to complex, both in phraseology and information'
(*Davies 1978: 17*)

'a progression from what seems simple and easy to the learner towards what appears to be harder because more complex, although of course several other factors have also to be taken account of'
(*Lee 1977: 248*)

Lee's definition seems to us the most satisfactory, for two reasons. Firstly, it emphasizes that grading needs to be approached *from the point of view of the L2 learner*. This should remind us that we can only judge the difficulty that our students may experience by actually trying material out with them. The other two definitions make no reference to the learner and at least imply that establishing the optimal sequence for learning is a question of objective fact.

Secondly, Lee allows for factors *apart from the language itself* that can contribute to the learners' perception of difficulty. Mackey seems to take account only of linguistic form; Davies's definition encompasses both form (phraseology) and content (information). But, as we stressed in Section One, listening difficulty can be a product of the interaction between the text, the listener, and the context in which listening takes place. We will now consider ways in which different course writers have dealt with the issue of grading.

6.2 Grading through text characteristics

Authors who have graded listening comprehension material in terms of text factors mention three main criteria: the level of difficulty of vocabulary, the complexity of syntax, and the duration of the recordings. The choice of each of these factors needs to be examined critically.

Vocabulary

The 'level' of vocabulary may be less relevant as a factor of difficulty in listening than one might think. In fact, the whole notion of 'level' of intrinsic difficulty of vocabulary is debatable (see McCarthy: *Vocabulary*, forthcoming in this Scheme).

We need to bear in mind that, in describing a particular L2 lexical item as *difficult*, people often mean that it is relatively *unusual*. But the frequency patterns in native and non-native contexts may be quite different. Some words, such as 'dustbin' ('trashcan' in North American English), are unusual only in the sort of language texts that L2 learners meet in coursebooks. Conversely, the word 'dictionary' is probably more common in the L2 learning context than it is in speech among native users.

It would be unreasonable to claim that 'dustbin' was in any sense more difficult than 'dictionary' simply because it was less common. What makes a new item difficult for learners is going to depend on a number of factors: the context in which they meet it; their knowledge of the topic; the word's analysability in terms of their L2 knowledge (e.g. dustbin → dust + bin); any similarity to an L1 item, and so on. Novelty cannot be equated with difficulty.

▶ TASK 65

The extract below comes from the introduction to a course in listening and note-taking (Ferguson and O'Reilly 1977). The authors say the book is intended for use 'by both native speakers of English and intermediate and advanced students of English as a foreign language'.

The Difficulty of the Extracts

All but the shortest talks have been rated for difficulty on a seven-point scale as follows:

Difficulty	Style	Example
1	very easy	comic
2	easy	
3	fairly easy	popular
4	standard	
5	fairly difficult	quality
6	difficult	academic
7	very difficult	scientific

(*Ferguson and O'Reilly 1977: 6*)

1 Look at the 'Style' and 'Example' columns. What seem to be the factors behind the setting of the levels of difficulty for the listening texts?

2 From your experience, do both native speakers and foreign learners find comic texts very easy, and scientific ones very difficult?

3 Before deciding whether to use this listening course with a particular group of students, what would you want to know about:
  – the learners?
  – the listening texts?

One of Ferguson and O'Reilly's 'very difficult' texts is on the subject of the population explosion. But from our discussion of the listener's sources of information (cf. Figure 1 in **1.4**), we might expect that a non-native learner who is an economist or demographer would find that 'very difficult' text easier to interpret than many native listeners who do not share that background information.

In formal, transactional settings such as the academic lecture theatre L2 listeners' subject knowledge enables them to cope with lecturers' use of highly specialized 'difficult' lexis. But, as we saw in Chaudron's research (**4.3**), an informal aside or explanation, inserted to help the native listeners, may have exactly the opposite effect on foreign members of the audience.

They may be unable to exploit the good intentions of the lecturer who attempts to simplify by the use of everyday language—'It's out of true, in simple terms it will wobble about'—or of cultural references—'about the distance between the wickets on a cricket pitch' (examples from Hutchinson and Waters 1981).

Conversely, in informal conversation the L2 listeners' problems are often caused not by their partners' use of highly specific vocabulary, but rather their rough-and-ready use of generalized everyday words and phrases. So it is important not to equate the relative formality of a text with its relative difficulty.

Grammar

Using complexity of syntax as a grading criterion is also less straightforward than it might first appear. In presenting learners with what are intended to be grammatically 'simplified' versions of original texts, teachers and course writers may actually make the adapted texts more difficult to understand than the originals (Johnson 1982).

This can also happen when a materials writer uses scripted material as the basis for a listening task that in real life would involve spontaneously produced speech. One of the principal characteristics of extempore speech is that it is grammatically simpler (in a general sense) than written language. In discussing this from the point of view of the *speaker*, Bygate says 'it is easier for speakers to improvise if they use less complex syntax' (1987: 14). Similarly, the relatively simple structure of spoken language has advantages for the *listeners*, who have to perform under time pressure, just as the speaker does. Using samples of language produced in actual communication can help to make both text and task more realistic.

▶ TASK 66

Below are extracts from two sets of instructions to enable listeners to draw the map of the same island. Read each of them *once only*, without letting your eye backtrack at all. (This is to make it resemble listening, rather than reading).

Version A

> *Introduction.* This is a drawing of an island which is oval in shape, or egg-shaped. It contains a number of land features which are indicated by words not pictures.
>
> *Description.* In the middle of your paper draw a large oval, measuring roughly fifteen centimetres across, by about seven centimetres (or half its width) down.

(*Jordan 1982: 59*)

Version B

'Okay right I've got an island + a map of an island in front of me + and I'm going to tell you how to draw the island + and I want you to draw it on your paper + now um the island is in fact shaped rather like a baked potato + now as I said the island looks rather like a baked potato + and is about five inches in length + and about + has a diameter of about three inches + so the first thing if you could just draw that + could you just draw that kind of shape + that will give you the outline of the island'
(*from Lynch 1984*)

1 Which version do you think would be easier for a student listening once only to a recording of the text?

2 In terms of grammar, does one seem more complex than the other?

3 What elements in the two texts would you expect to cause difficulty for a non-native listener of, say, lower intermediate level?

Version B of the instructions in Task 66 was spoken by one native speaker of English to another, without rehearsal. Recordings of scripted texts often omit precisely the elements of spontaneous speech that may help to make it comprehensible—to native and non-native listeners alike. These elements include relative grammatical simplicity, e.g. the use of co-ordination ('and', 'but', 'so', etc.) as opposed to the subordination typically found in written texts (such as temporal and relative clauses). The contrasts between written and spoken language are discussed in detail in Bygate: *Speaking* (1987).

So the relationship between syntactic complexity and difficulty of comprehension is not a straightforward one. Its implications for language course syllabus design are dealt with in detail in Nunan: *Syllabus Design*, also published in this Scheme.

Length of text
The third of the factors that are conventionally employed as a means of grading texts is the duration of the recordings that students listen to. In this context the shortness of a particular text is believed to simplify the task of comprehension. One obvious reason for using length as a criterion is listener fatigue; another is the effect of memory load.

▶ TASK 67

This is an extract from the Introduction to a post-intermediate level EFL listening course (O'Neill and Scott 1974):

Each unit consists of a spontaneous, unscripted conversation of between four and a half and six minutes' duration. It is divided into

three or four parts. This is done to facilitate listening comprehension. We have found that listening of this kind should not exceed about one and a half minutes.
(*O'Neill and Scott 1974: v*)

1 In what way do you think the division into ninety-second segments actually makes listening easier than if the students had to hear the whole conversation?
2 Do you see any disadvantages in the authors' approach?

At first sight, it may seem natural to use recording duration as a means of grading: understanding six minutes' speech in a foreign language appears to be a more demanding task than understanding ninety seconds. But is it only a question of quantity? On reflection we can see that it is in fact illogical to argue that text length is, *in itself*, a critical factor of listening difficulty; 'the longer someone speaks on a topic the more chance there is of understanding the point of what he is trying to say' (Wallace 1983: 106).

Moreover, as we saw in Tasks 43 and 44, when native speakers are talking to L2 listeners of limited proficiency, one of the ways in which they modify what they say is to produce *more* words than in native-native conversation. So the speaker's natural way of making speech easier to understand for a foreign listener is to make various adjustments that result in longer, not shorter, stretches of language.

▶ TASK 68

Relatively few listening course writers clearly explain the specific factors that they have used to grade recorded material. Blundell and Stokes, in *Task Listening*, are among the few who do:

'The units have been ordered according to the length of recording, the number and speed of speakers and the type of task.'
(*Blundell and Stokes 1981: vii*)

Table 1 overleaf gives the data from the course's Teacher's Book for the first five and last five units. As you will see, they include only three of their stated grading factors, disregarding speed of speaking.

Table 1: Grading factors in *Task Listening*

Unit	Length	Speakers	Task
1	1.40	1	grid completion
2	1.25	1	'balloon' filling
3	1.09	1*	map marking
4	2.10	1	match tape with pictures
5	1.20	2	making notes
22 (a)	0.30	2	match tape with pictures
(b)	1.05	2	,, ,, ,, ,,
(c)	0.27	2	,, ,, ,, ,,
(d)	0.45	2	,, ,, ,, ,,
23 (a)	0.50	2	,, ,, ,, ,,
(b)	0.30	2	,, ,, ,, ,,
(c)	0.40	2	,, ,, ,, ,,
24	2.01	2	picture selection (1 from 4)
25	2.48	2	identifying differences
26	2.03		picture selection (2 from 8)

*Unit 3 has two speakers, but not in conversation; a newsreader announces the weather forecast, which is then given by the weatherman.

Can you see a consistent pattern in the ordering of the units—in terms either of the text length, or of the other factors mentioned?

Clearly, there are some types of listening where length *is* a source of difficulty—for example, taking notes in a fifty-minute lecture, where physical tiredness can cause our attention to wander, so that we miss parts of the talk. But the degree to which the length of a listening text actually causes problems will vary according to other factors, especially our overall listening purpose, as we saw in **2.5**.

In **4** we summarized research into other factors that have been investigated and found to be significant causes of difficulty in listening. Those we discussed were:

information organization
familiarity of topic
explicitness of information
– redundancy
– sufficiency of information
– referring expressions
type of input

As far as we are aware, none of them has so far been used in a principled and explicit way by designers of listening comprehension materials. In **7** we present extracts from our own classroom materials, in which these factors did form the basis for grading difficulty.

6.3 Grading through task factors

The earlier tendency of materials writers to be preoccupied with text factors reflected a contemporary concern in linguistics with describing the *form* of language—the 'what' of language. It seemed feasible to identify measurable elements in a piece of spoken language and take them into account to grade their order of appearance in a language course: the statistical frequency of the lexical items; the complexity of the grammatical structures; the length of the recording. The overall level of listening difficulty could (it was supposed) then be calculated in a relatively mechanical way and marked on a scale, as in the imaginary example below:

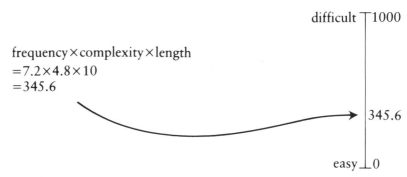

frequency × complexity × length
$$= 7.2 \times 4.8 \times 10$$
$$= 345.6$$

Figure 4: An index of text difficulty

(This whole approach to establishing text difficulty was essentially that adopted earlier in relation to reading texts; for discussion of such 'readability formulae', see Wallace: *Reading*, forthcoming in this series).

Listening purpose

More recently, attention has been focused on the social and communicative *function* of language—what we might call the 'why' of language. So one of the features of the discussion and design of listening comprehension materials over the last ten years or so has been the development of ways of grading the difficulty of the task by manipulating and adjusting the listener's purpose.

▶ TASK 69

In a section entitled 'Purpose and expectation', Ur (1984: 4) says 'It would seem a good idea when presenting a listening passage in class to give the students some information about the content, situation and speaker(s) before they actually start listening.'

Before considering the questions below, look back to Figure 1 in **1.4**.

1 Do you agree with Ur? Why (not)?

2 Would it be advisable to give the learners *all* the information beforehand, rather than some of it?

3 Would you want to include in the pre-listening information all the vocabulary items that you know the learners have never encountered before?

In theory, at least, it is possible to take any listening text and compose a listening task that would be appropriately difficult for a particular group of learners at any level of L2 proficiency. Windeatt (1981), for example, produced a set of listening exercises intended for self-access use, in which the individual learners could decide for themselves which of six levels of task difficulty they wished to work at (1 = least demanding; 6 = hardest).

▶ TASK 70

Below are Windeatt's instructions for three different levels of task. They represent his levels 5, 3, and 1, but are presented here in jumbled order. Read each set of instructions (A, B, and C) and think about the demands that they make on the listener.

Set A: Level ?

1. Listen to one of the news items and try to write down the main points.
2. Listen to one of the news items and try to write down as many of the words as you can.

Set B: Level ?

1. Listen to the whole news broadcast once and write down as much as you can remember.
2. Listen to the broadcast and stop at the end of each item. Make a summary of the main points.
3. Listen to one or more of the news items and write down all of the words.

Set C: Level ?

1. How many news items are there?
2. Is there an item about the weather?
3. Is there just one person reading the news, or do other people give reports of interviews as well?

Which set corresponds to which level?

Windeatt's materials are unusual because of the range of task difficulty they provide for a single text. They show that it is in principle possible to 'grade the task, not the text'—to use any text and to create listening tasks at a level appropriate to particular students. In practice, most published comprehension materials appear to aim for some sort of balance between text factors and task factors—represented by the dotted line in Figure 5—combining the two scales of difficulty that we have discussed in this unit.

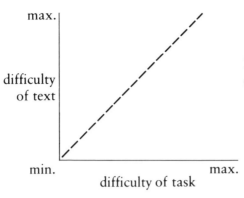

Figure 5: Balancing the difficulty of text and task

Response required
In **5.7** we referred to the range of comprehension exercises currently in use in listening materials. They represent the *external* response required of the learner. But the level of *internal* response is related to how closely the response expected from the learner resembles that of the original listener.

We have said a task can be designed in such a way that the learner is required to act as an observer/eavesdropper, or as a participant. A participant task such as following instructions is likely to be easier (and perhaps more interesting) if the spoken text was recorded under conditions similar to those in which the learners hear the cassette.

We might take the map texts from Task 66 as an example. Both required the same outcome, the drawing of the island. One was scripted by a course designer, for an actor to read into a microphone in a recording studio. The other was spoken extempore by someone engaged in an act of communication with a listener who was actually trying to sketch the island.

If the L2 listeners' response is to be similar to that of the original listener, the listening text should contain a degree of help comparable to that which would be available to the real-life listener.

▶ TASK 71

The two exercises below are similar. In both cases, the learners' task is to mark a route on a map printed in their listening course book.

Think about what effect the following would have on the speaker's performance if this were a real-life conversation:

1 listener's relationship with the speaker

2 the physical setting

3 local knowledge

Listening task A (Blundell and Stokes 1981)
An English motorist gets lost on her way to visit a friend in Oxford. She telephones her to get help. She has no map.

Listening task B (Stokes 1984)
The listener is a French driver who gets lost in a British town. He stops a passer-by and asks the way to a specific street. He has no map.

After considering factors 1–3, which of the two texts do you think would be more likely to offer the most help to an L2 listener *if recorded spontaneously.*

Support material
This is perhaps the aspect of listening comprehension courses that has altered most over the last ten years or so. There has been a visible change, literally, in the form in which listening activities are presented to the learner. Looking through courses published before, say, 1980, you find that most of the space is taken up with printed text: introductions, explanations of vocabulary, comprehension questions, and perhaps follow-up activities. More recently, there has been a dramatic increase in the amount of non-verbal material used as support for listening tasks. Why?

The increased use of non-verbal support material (illustrations, photographs, grids, graphs, etc.) in listening activities is largely the result of a growing concern with helping learners to focus their attention on the relevant information in the recorded text rather than distracting their attention with potentially confusing printed information. The fact that the human listener is a 'limited processor' (see **4.1**) makes it essential that the printed information should be (1) relevant and (2) not so excessive as to be distracting. We do not want learners to fail in listening activities because they are hampered by reading difficulties.

▶ TASK 72

Below are two listening exercises, both based on interviews with people talking about their jobs. The first is with a postman and the second with a railwayman. Consider the two exercises and the extent to which the arrangement of the information guides (or limits) the learners' comprehension.

Exercise A

> 1. The postman had expected to work ..... every day
>   **A** from 8.30 a.m. to 4.00 p.m.
>   **B** from 8.00 a.m. to 4.30 p.m.
>   **C** from 8.30 a.m. to 4.30 p.m.
>   **D** from 4.30 a.m. to 8.30 p.m.

(*Underwood 1971: 24*)

Exercise B
(The extract is of a railwayman talking about shift work.)

Exercise D		Listen to the Extract again and complete the chart below.			
Sun	2 5 p.m.–2 a.m.	9 –	16	23	
Mon	3 10 p.m.–6 a.m.	10 2 p.m.–10 p.m.	17	24	
Tue	4	11	18	25	
Wed	5	12	19	26	
Thu	6	13	20	27	
Fri	7	14	21	28	
Sat	8	15	22	29	

Now answer the following questions.

1 Can Jack go to his sister's for supper at 8 p.m. on Thursday, 20th?
2 Can he take his family to visit relatives for the evening on Sunday, 23rd?
3 Can he go shopping with his wife on Wednesday, 12th?
4 Can he go to the cinema on Friday, 21st?

(*Underwood and Barr 1980: 31*)

1 Which exercise do you think is the more demanding, and why?

2 Can you see any connection between the format of the two exercises and the dates of publication of the two courses?

It is important to remember that graphics are not necessarily simpler than words. Particular forms of visual material, such as maps or statistical line graphs, may require a substantial amount of familiarization with their general conventions, as well as with their specific details. So time needs to be spent on helping learners to interpret and absorb such material before the listening activity begins.

Support material for listening is not restricted to diagrams; it may be verbal or pictorial too. Transcripts and vocabulary lists are two traditional forms of support for listening comprehension exercises, but they are not without their problems. It is possible to argue that transcript material should be used in early stages of a unit or a course, then gradually reduced to help the listeners to be more reliant on their ears than their eyes. Conversely, you can argue that transcript material should only be made available at the end of a sequence of activities, as the source that students refer to for confirmation of their solutions to exercises.

▶ TASK 73

This sequence of listening tasks comes from a lecture comprehension and note-taking course (James, Jordan, and Matthews 1979). In each unit, the learners work through three stages of listening activities, with varying types of visual support, and progressively longer listening texts, as shown below. Read through the descriptions and then consider the questions that follow.

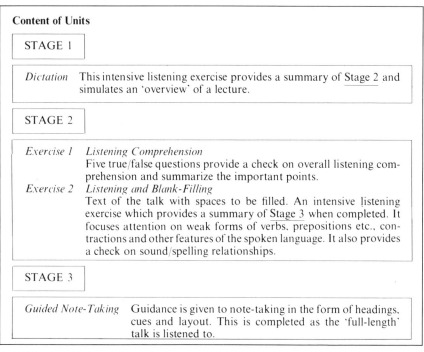

Content of Units

STAGE 1

Dictation   This intensive listening exercise provides a summary of Stage 2 and simulates an 'overview' of a lecture.

STAGE 2

Exercise 1   *Listening Comprehension*
Five true/false questions provide a check on overall listening comprehension and summarize the important points.
Exercise 2   *Listening and Blank-Filling*
Text of the talk with spaces to be filled. An intensive listening exercise which provides a summary of Stage 3 when completed. It focuses attention on weak forms of verbs, prepositions etc., contractions and other features of the spoken language. It also provides a check on sound/spelling relationships.

STAGE 3

Guided Note-Taking   Guidance is given to note-taking in the form of headings, cues and layout. This is completed as the 'full-length' talk is listened to.

(*James, Jordan, and Matthews 1979: 7–8*)

1 Why is there no support material at Stage 1?

2 The Stage 2/1 task provides different support material from that available to the learner at Stage 2/2. Why have the authors structured the listening in this way? Bear in mind the focus of the two exercises.

Task difficulty can be influenced not only by the type of support material the learner has available, but also by the amount. In designing listening exercises, one has to take account of the fact that, if the support material is verbal rather than visual, there is a risk of turning the activity into one that practises reading comprehension skills, not listening.

▶ TASK 74

Here is an extract from the guided note-taking materials referred to at Stage 3 in Task 73. As you will see, it includes the use of abbreviations which have been explained earlier in the course.

How could you make the learner's Stage 3 task either easier, or more difficult, by altering this support material?

Unit 3   Stage 3   Guided Note-Taking

Complete the following as you listen to the Stage 3 talk.

Title: . . . .

4 most   :

  1   Understand what lecturer says . . . .

      cannot. . . . .

      Often poss. to understand much by . . . .

      . . . .

  2   What's imp.?

      Most imp. info. = ... make sure . . . .

                        . . . .

                  implies . . . .

            Good lecturer . . . .

            . . . . or . . . . signals

            Explicit = write it down!

            Indirect = ... or . . . . etc.

                  = sth. imp.

                  . . . .

                  . . . .

                  = sth. incidental

(James, Jordan, and Matthews 1979: 31)

Our summary (in **4**) of research findings about task-related factors of listening difficulty included four influential factors:

processing load
– pre-listening activity to provide purpose
– time available
visual support
listener grouping
type of task

In published EFL materials, writers have concentrated mainly on the first two of these factors in grading and sequencing listening comprehension materials. As far as we are aware, no courses address the last two factors in an explicit way—i.e. by a method that they *describe and explain* to the teachers using the material. In **7** we illustrate how we have attempted to incorporate all four factors into experimental classroom materials and to explain the grading principles to teachers.

6.4 Grading complexity, or the complexity of grading

Summarizing **6.2** and **6.3**, we could say that the whole issue of grading difficulty has become progressively more complex. The index of text difficulty (Figure 4) was an over-simplification, because it assumed that comprehension problems were linguistic. Taking task/context-related factors into account resulted in a fuller picture (Figure 5). But even this two-way representation of difficulty, where both text and task factors come into play, still amounts to an underestimate of the complexity of establishing the overall level of difficulty experienced in understanding a specific text for a particular purpose.

Brown and Yule (1983a) have suggested that four principal groups of factors need to be taken into account in creating graded programmes of oral language skills. Each of these is not a single entity, as earlier labels such as 'text' and 'task' would suggest, but a mixture of component factors:

speaker—number of speakers, speed of speech, accent
listener—eavesdropper or participant, required level of response, individual interest in the topic
content—grammar, vocabulary, information structure, assumed background knowledge
support—physical objects, visual aids (including video), and printed texts.

This is clearly a more comprehensive view of grading than is provided under the 'text or task' perspective. We will offer an analogy that may help to capture the complexity. Think of the control panel in a recording studio. The recording engineers have in front of them a set of slide controls which they can adjust to any point between zero and maximum. Each of the slides contributes to the desired blend of voices, instruments, pre-recorded background noises and so on.

For Brown and Yule, there are four main slide controls. Each of these can be set at any point, independently of the precise setting of the other slides, as in the diagram below:

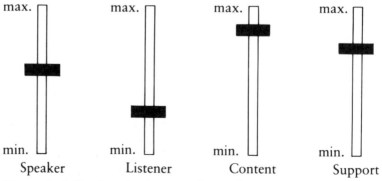

Figure 6: Adjusting the factors of complexity

We have to bear in mind that each of these slide controls represents a combination of factors. For example, in deciding the level at which you should set the 'speaker' control, you have to consider the relevant component factors: how many speakers are actively involved in the text, the speed at which some of them (those participants whose ideas and comments you want the learners to focus on) talk to each other, and the likely familiarity of their accents for your students.

The emerging picture is certainly complex, but our view is that it is better to confront the complexities involved and to work out listening programmes that take account of as many likely or proven factors of difficulty as possible, than simply to present learners with an apparently arbitrary collection of listening passages in random order, as many course writers still do. In Brown's words:

> Comprehension teaching at the moment … is very much a hit-or-miss affair. The student is presented with a text associated with some task and told to get on with the task. If the task is not performed very well, and there is not some patent problem arising from a 'language point', there is little the teacher can do but give the assignment a low mark and tell the student to 'do better next time'.
> (*Brown 1986b: 286*)

Even those authors who recognize a need to grade the learners' experience of listening difficulty seem to be rather ambivalent about the issue. Compare these statements (co-)written by the same author:

> The units have been ordered according to the length of the recording, the number and speed of speakers and the type of task. Bearing this in mind the teacher is free to use the units in any order.
> (*Blundell and Stokes 1981: vii*)

> The units are not arranged in any particular order of difficulty. However, students will find those units which occur towards the beginning of the book are generally shorter or more straightforward than later ones. Reference to the Teacher's Book and cassette will help determine the order which best suits your students.
> (*Stokes 1984: vii*)

▶ TASK 75

1 Do you see any conflict between these statements?

2 Is there a contradiction within each of them?

3 How, in your view, should teachers determine the order which best suits their particular students?

The impression one gets from reading introductions to listening materials is often unclear. If teachers are to take the sort of active role in the development of classroom practice that this series of books is encouraging, then they need as much information as possible about what underlies the construction and ordering of tasks.

In 7 we will be illustrating our own proposals for making such information available. We present samples from an experimental series of listening materials which attempt to take teachers 'behind the scenes' of task design. As well as providing the sample materials themselves, we explain the principles on which our comprehension tasks are based. In this way, we aim to enable you to assess whether those grading principles might be relevant to your own teaching, either in creating graded sequences of published materials or in designing your own tasks.

7 Samples from a graded listening programme

7.1 Introduction

In this part of the book we present sample materials intended to put into practice the sort of grading principles that we have discussed in **4** and **6**. We explain the detailed construction of specific listening materials and activities. The tasks provide an opportunity for you (1) to get first-hand experience of the comprehension materials; (2) to analyse the grading system behind the task/materials design, and (3) to evaluate the performances of L1 and L2 listeners using the materials.

7.2 Background to the materials

The materials were originally designed as part of an L1 listening comprehension project (summarized in Brown, Anderson, Shadbolt, and Lynch 1987). The principal aim of the project was to investigate the relative degree of comprehension difficulty experienced by teenage native listeners trying to understand different types of spoken language under various conditions. This led to the production of materials designed to develop listening comprehension; these materials were tried out with the original L1 listeners and subsequently with adult foreign learners of English.

Purpose

The materials that we will be presenting here have to be seen as a sample, in two senses. Firstly, for reasons of space, we can illustrate only part of our series of materials. But we hope they will convey both a general impression of the approach we adopted and also give some insight into the details of the design. Secondly, and more importantly—the primary purpose of the original materials was to show teachers ways of constructing comprehension tasks based on reasoned grading. So they were to serve teachers as a template, not a blueprint. In other words, the aim was to explain how and why the programme was designed as it was, enabling teachers to understand the 'nuts and bolts' of grading comprehension tasks. As we stressed in **6**, satisfactory explanations have rarely been offered by materials designers.

Overview of the materials

The programme was designed within Brown and Yule's grading framework (Figure 3 in **4.3**) and included tasks based on both *static* and *dynamic* types of input. We will be describing and explaining the design principles underlying three sets of materials: 'Diagrams' and 'Maps' (static) and 'Narratives' (dynamic). As you will see, the grading factors applied in our materials are among those suggested by the experimental studies reviewed in Section One.

Teaching procedure

In the case of the static tasks, the materials comprised four elements:

a hearer's version (plan, diagram, or map) which the students were required to mark or amend in some way

a cassette containing recorded instructions which, if followed correctly, allowed the listeners to complete their task

a speaker's version for the teacher to refer to, showing the solution to the students' task

a set of guidelines indicating the likely/intended points of difficulty.

Problem points

The static tasks were designed to confront listeners with a number of 'problem points'—points in the spoken text where they might be unsure which item on their task-sheet (e.g. which shop in a street plan) was being referred to. In the first two sets of tasks, the location of the problem points was indicated by buzzes on the tape; after a buzz, the teacher stopped the cassette to allow the pupils time to decide whether they needed additional information. The listeners had a four-way choice at each buzz. They could:

1 ask the teacher to play on (either if there was no problem, or if they thought the next part of the recording might help them solve a problem)

2 get the tape replayed if they were not sure what had been said

3 ask the teacher for more information to help them out of the difficulty

4 get a listener who believed they had solved the problem to explain their solution.

When any pupil felt they needed more precise information, or wanted to hear the section again, this had to be discussed and agreed by the group as a whole, before the teacher would respond to the request. Here, the intention was to establish an atmosphere of co-operation rather than competition. We had designed the problem points so that, in most cases, at least some pupils would feel a need for assistance, while others would see how to resolve the difficulty without having to get more information from the teacher.

▶ ## TASK 76

One reason for getting the listeners to discuss the problems was to minimize competitiveness within the group. What other advantages might there be in allowing the students to compare and discuss their comprehension difficulties, rather than being told the correct answer by their teacher? (It may be helpful to think about L1 and L2 teaching separately.)

Our plan was therefore to allow those who needed assistance to get it first from other listeners with access to the same information, rather than relying straight away on the usual source of authority, the teacher. (The classroom norm is, of course, that the teacher 'knows the answers'; for discussion of this, see Wright: *Roles of Teachers and Learners*, in this Scheme.)

Classroom trials
As explained earlier, the original target audience were Scottish secondary school pupils. The materials were tried out with some 200 fourteen-year-old native listeners, across a wide range of academic ability. Later we carried out a smaller-scale pilot study with thirty adult foreign learners of English at varying levels of L2 proficiency, from post-elementary to advanced. All were following a full-time general-purpose English course and in all three groups there was a variety of native languages.

In both L1 and L2 classrooms, the listeners' performances were audiotaped for later transcription and analysis. You will have the chance in some of the tasks in this unit to see extracts from our transcripts of the performances of eight groups of learners: groups A–F (native users of English), and groups G–I (adult foreign learners of English).

▶   TASK 77

1 Do you think that post-elementary, intermediate, and advanced level EFL students could usefully tackle the same listening texts and tasks, with the same instructions?

2 Would you expect the lower-proficiency students to experience greater difficulties than the more advanced learners:
   – in the language skills required to understand the text, e.g. vocabulary, knowledge of syntax?
   – in the listening skills, e.g. knowing when/how to make reasonable assumptions; knowing that a single thing can be referred to in a variety of ways; knowing how to ask clarification questions?

Summary
The aim of the L1 study was to see if it was possible to develop native pupils' ability both to recognize comprehension problems as they arose and to take appropriate action, either through questions to each other or, when necessary, to the teacher. Ultimately, we hoped that they would transfer this successful listening behaviour to other classrooms, with teachers of other subjects, not just in English lessons and using these materials.

The main question we wanted the L2 pilot study to answer was: Can these materials be used in the L2 classroom, or are they simply too difficult for some levels of foreign listener? We will be asking you to evaluate some of the evidence from the classroom performances.

7.3 Diagrams

In this series of five tasks, the listeners are asked to draw various figures according to instructions spoken on tape. By way of introduction to the material, we are going to ask you to try out one of the activities yourself. Obviously, since you have the material in printed form rather than on cassette, we have to adapt the comprehension activity. We suggest two ways of using the material, depending on whether you are reading this book by yourself, or are using it with a group of colleagues or fellow students.

Method A. If you are working alone, you should do the task as a *reading comprehension* exercise. Read the Instructions tapescript and complete the task accordingly. Do not look at the Speaker's version of the task item—printed as an Appendix at the end of the book—until you have completed the comprehension exercise.

Method B. If you are working with a group, you can carry out the task with a partner, as a *paired speaking/listening* activity. The speaker should read the Instructions tapescript, exactly as printed in the book; the listener carries out the task according to the spoken instructions. When problems arise, the listener is free to stop and question the speaker, asking for clarification. The speaker may also refer to the Guidelines and the Speaker's version of the completed diagram or map in the Appendix at the back of the book.

▶ TASK 78

Try out the Diagram 2 task, using either Method A or Method B. The starting point is a partly drawn figure, which you have to complete according to the instructions you will read (Method A) or hear (Method B).

Hearer's version

Cigarette consumption by adults in Scotland

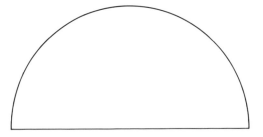

Instructions tapescript

'right diagram two + diagram two is about the number of cigarettes that Scottish adults smoke a day so what you should have to start with is a circle with a line across the middle (*pause*) and the first thing you should do is to draw a line from the centre of the circle down to the bottom (*pause*) so now you've got two quarters at the bottom of the circle and outside them you put "25%" (*pause*) um then you go up to the top half of the circle you've got to draw a line from the centre at an angle and the line should go + should + the line should end up about a third of the way up between the side of the circle and the top of the circle (*pause*) right then the next thing + um + is to draw another line + again from the centre + and this time you draw it up at an angle to the other side about half-way between the side of the circle and the top (*pause*) OK so now you've er you've er you've got the top half of the circle divided into three slices + that + you've got a big one a medium one and a small one and outside those you put "8%" "12%" and "30%" (*pause*) right inside the circle + inside the slices + you've now got to write in what each of them er represents (*pause*) so inside the two at the bottom + in one of them you put "less than 20 per day" and in the other you put "20–30 per day" (*pause*) then up at the top again in the 12% one you put "have stopped smoking" and in the other two you put "do not smoke" and "over 30 per day" (*pause*) right and then you're finished'

► TASK 79

1 If you used Method B, what listening comprehension difficulties, if any, did you experience as you tried to complete Task 78?

2 If you used Method A, look back to the Instructions tapescript. Which points would be unclear or ambiguous if you had heard them, rather than read them?

3 Whether you used Method A or B, compare your answers to question 1 or 2 with our intended 'problem points', shown in the Diagram 2 Guidelines (Appendix 1 at the end of the book).

The Diagram series consists of five tasks, designed to create a 'slope' of increasing comprehension difficulty. The factors we used to grade difficulty included one we had already used in an earlier series in the listening programme (explicitness of information) and two further factors: the amount of support material, and the type of figure involved.

Amount of visual support

In designing the series, we assumed it is easier to complete the details of a figure whose outer shape is already drawn on paper for you, than when only part of that outline is provided. For example, we assumed that completing the inner details of a square would be simpler when that square is on your sheet of paper than when you also have to draw the square itself. The starting point for Diagram 1 was a fully drawn square; in Diagrams 2 and 3, the listeners had to complete a partially drawn figure; and in Diagram tasks 4 and 5, they had to draw a figure from scratch.

Type of figure

It seems likely that being told in advance that the shape of the diagram is a conventional one, such as a circle or triangle, makes it easier for the listener to picture the finished product than when the final figure is a less familiar shape.

Explicitness of information—referring expressions

The spoken instructions for the Diagram and earlier series were scripted, to confront listeners with 'problem points' where they have to make decisions about whether to ask for additional information, because the recorded instructions use particular referring expressions that are (intentionally) unclear.

Firstly, an instruction might be *ambiguous*. For example, in Diagram 2 the speaker refers to 'the other two' segments of the pie-chart, which should leave listeners uncertain as to which one they are to label 'do not smoke' and which one 'over 30 per day'. They are intended to recognize the need either to ask which of the two is which, or to apply their knowledge of Scottish smoking habits.

The second type of instruction involved a degree of *contradiction*. One of the most difficult aspects of comprehension is knowing how best to deal with new information that actually contradicts your own picture of how things are. In Diagrams 3 and 5, the listeners were faced with situations of that sort. This practice in dealing with contradictions was designed to lead on to the solution of similar conflicts in the Map tasks that made up the next series in the listening programme.

Summary of grading

Three factors of grading were incorporated into the design of the five Diagram series tasks: the amount of visual support; the type of diagram involved, and the explicitness of information (ambiguity and contradiction). These are shown in Table 2.

Having now given you first-hand experience of an example of the materials in the Diagram series and described the intended grading factors, we turn to the issue that concerns the teacher most: how did they work in the classroom?

	Grading factors			
			Referring expressions	
Task no.	Completeness of diagram	Type of diagram	Ambiguity	Contradiction
1	complete	abstract	yes	no
2	partial	representational	yes	no
3	partial	abstract	yes	yes
4	none	representational	yes	no
5	none	abstract	yes	yes

Table 2: Grading in the Diagram series

L1 listeners' performances

We will be presenting transcript extracts from classroom performances by the L1 and L2 listeners referred to in **7.2**. You will be asked to use these extracts in two ways: (1) to *analyse* the skills demanded by Diagram task 2; (2) to *evaluate* the listeners' success (or lack of it) in applying the relevant skills.

The L1 and L2 recordings have been transcribed in slightly different ways. As the L1 classes were larger than the L2 groups, it was impossible for us to identify the owners of individual voices from the tape. So sequences of L1 pupils' comments are grouped together as '**Ps**', with different individual comments separated by an oblique stroke '/'. In both sets of transcripts, the other symbols used are '**Tp**' for the taped instructions and '**Te**' for comments by the teacher.

▶ TASK 80

Read the extracts below, from two native groups tackling the pie-chart task.

Group D

Tp: 'you've got the top half of the circle divided into three slices + that + you've got a big one, a medium one and a small one and outside these you put "8%" "12%" and "30%" '

Ps: stop / the wee one?

Te: use your common sense obviously 8% 12% it's self-evident which one is which

Ps: that one is 8 and that one is 12 / what's the big one? / 30%? / 30

Te: 8% 12% 30%

Tp: 'inside the slices you've now got to write what each of them represents + so inside the two at the bottom in one of them you put "less than 20 per day" and in the other you put "20–30 per day" '

P: stop which side is it?

Te: it doesn't in this case matter which + you can see that because they're equal size

Group E

Tp: (*as above*) '. . . "8%" "12%" and "30%" '

Ps: which direction? / it's kind of obvious is it not? / I mean they're different sizes / so the largest is . . . / we'll add it up that's 100 / em it all adds up to 100 / it's 20 and 30 and that's 50 and 50 it's 100 . . . / right all agreed 'cos that's the small one which is 8, the medium 12 and the big 30 / quite hard to understand, that one eh? (*sarcastic tone of voice*)

Te: (*as before*) . . . '20–30 per day'

Ps: so it's less then / need to hear it again / is it in the quarters or is it in this bit? / it's in the quarters / so it's less than 20 . . . / now do you think it matters which? / no / no 'cos they're exactly the same, aren't they? / right everybody got that in? / so that's less than 20 a day that means that'll be less than 10 a day will it not / we'll find out / it might be more

Can you find evidence in those two extracts of pupils' ability to:

1 recognize ambiguous instructions

2 respond appropriately by asking questions

3 specify what information they need

4 use other sources of knowledge/information to support their listening?

Generally speaking, most pupils were quite competent at recognizing when an instruction did not provide enough unambiguous information to allow them to complete their current task. But among a minority these comprehension monitoring skills seemed less well developed. They allowed far too many underspecified instructions to pass unchallenged, despite repeated prompting from the teacher about whether they needed to ask for the tape to be replayed, or for more information. As a result, the group of pupils who performed in this way were unable to complete their task-sheets successfully. (These performances were therefore reminiscent of those of much younger listeners, in the studies reported in **2.4**, who were shown to have similar difficulties in responding appropriately to inadequate messages.)

Although most of the pupils were good at monitoring their comprehension and indicating any difficulty, they varied in how well they specified their problem and in how effectively they asked questions to elicit the additional information they required.

Another difference among the responses of various groups was in their ability to apply background knowledge to assist in solving the problems the tasks were designed to present. Some listeners seem to be more able, or more willing, to go beyond the information supplied in the instructions to help their comprehension of a message.

Some listeners use not only relevant *factual knowledge* but also their familiarity with the particular type of discourse (diagrams, pie-charts, maps) that the task exemplifies. In terms of Figure 1 (**1.4**), they use their *procedural knowledge* and their knowledge of the current *listening context*, in addition to their knowledge of the world and the language system.

▶ ## TASK 81

Look again at the transcript extracts in Task 80.

1 Which of the two L1 groups makes better use of their knowledge of the conventions of diagrams?

2 Would you want to make any comment on *when* and *how* the teacher of group D contributes to the activity?

Group E's performance shows quite a sophisticated level of listening skill and relies on the pupils' use of several different kinds of listener knowledge. Moreover, such knowledge has to be deployed flexibly; they recognize that they need not get the underspecified instruction 'inside the two at the bottom' clarified. Group D do not respond as effectively on this point and it is in fact the teacher who does the interpretative work for them, by her final explanatory comment.

L2 listeners' performances

In general we were very impressed by the way the L2 listeners tackled the tasks. It is worth recalling that the comprehension materials they worked on were identical to those used with the L1 pupils; they had not been adapted or simplified in any way. Nevertheless, with varying amounts of effort in discussion, questioning, and replaying of the cassette, the three groups at widely differing levels (post-elementary group G, intermediate group H, and post-intermediate/advanced group I) coped with problems such as ambiguous or underspecified descriptions.

On occasions, like some L1 pupils, a group would allow too much input to pass by unquestioned. In one case, Group H allowed a complete set of instructions to finish before one of them finally said 'Sorry, I didn't catch'. But this sort of ineffective listening was the exception. Generally the L2 learners seemed to adopt good active listening strategies: attempting to build an interpretation of the spoken input as they heard each item; checking whether they understood what they were required to do; discussing and asking questions when uncertainties arose.

In the L2 recordings, unlike those of the L1 groups, we were able to recognize which students had said what, because of the smaller group size.

So the transcripts usually assign each comment to the appropriate speaker.
Where a number of the students spoke at the same time, this is shown as
'**Ss**'; otherwise the letters refer to individual students.

▶ ## TASK 82

Look through the extracts for evidence that these L2 learners are
able to:

1 use sources of information *beyond* what they hear, to help their
   listening

2 make effective use of group discussion.

Group G
Tp: '. . . and in the other two (*30% and 8% segments*) you put "do
    not smoke" and "over 30 per day" '
O: I guess the 30% must be 'do not smoke'
E: you supppose + your imagination is good but the tape don't
    said
O: I think the 30% don't smoke and 8% over 30
Ss: no / no / yes
E: the tape don't said . . .
O: but you have two parts eh? one part is 30% and the other is 8%
    + you have two categories + no smokers + and smokers upper
S: 30
E: smokers up 30 cigarettes a day + the no smokers are the 30% or
    the 8%
A: we don't know
I: ask the teacher
Te: 'do not smoke' is 30%
O: yes!
E: it's obvious!

Group H
Tp: '. . . so inside the two at the bottom + + in one of them you put
    "less than 20 per day" '
S: which one? excuse me
Tp: 'and in the other you put "20–30 per day" '
Ss: which one?
Y: any one + any one because
A: we don't care + 25 each
Y: because
B: same
A: it's the same

Part of the improvement observable across the L2 students' performances
is their greater use of various types of knowledge, beyond what is explicitly

stated. There is also evidence of listeners becoming aware of different listening strategies as they tackle the tasks; asking each other questions, debating the possible solutions suggested in the group, making inferences based on topical or discourse-type knowledge, waiting for later information in the task instructions, and so on.

It was the application of these various strategies that the materials were designed to encourage and develop. Our aim was to lead learners to the conscious realization that successful listening is both an *active* process requiring the use of multiple information sources and a *reciprocal* process requiring the listeners to query and react to the speaker (or text) as they listen.

The extracts in Task 82 seem to show that foreign listeners, like native listeners, can use their procedural knowledge of how language is used in certain types of discourse to assist in their listening, either (1) by excluding potential interpretations of a piece of ambiguous text, or (2) by deciding that in the particular context of part of a task the underspecification does not in fact represent a problem.

This need for flexible listening is a very important point for L2 listeners to become aware of. Even in the case of L1 listening, very many messages are potentially ambiguous and capable of various interpretations; in the L2 case, the listeners' incomplete grasp of the language may aggravate the problems of comprehension if they are unsure of the precise sense of the message. They must become sensitive to the relevance of particular problematic parts of the text for their current listening task.

7.4 Maps

The three tasks in the Map series developed the types of comprehension practised in the earlier series. The listeners were presented with a map on which they had to mark a route, according to recorded instructions. Their map matched, to varying degrees, one being used by the speaker; the degree of difference between the two versions increased over the three tasks.

▶ TASK 83

This is the first of the three Map tasks. It involves the map of a city called Tai Tu. As in Task 78, you should use either Method A (reading comprehension) or Method B (paired speaking/listening).

Tai Tu City Tour: Introduction
'The map you have in front of you shows part of the city centre of Tai Tu, in the Far East. As you listen, mark in the route that your tour will take. You are staying at the hotel in the centre of the map and your tour will begin and end there.

If you are not sure of the route as the guide explains it, ask for the tape to be stopped. You can then hear that part of the tape replayed, or you can ask for more information to help you.'

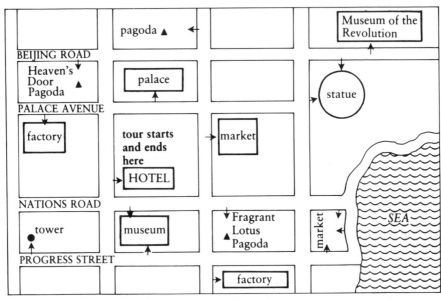

(Arrows on map indicate position of entrances to places of interest)

Hearer's map

Instructions tapescript
'right + the tour starts off from the hotel + and we go up as far as the Beijing Road + we turn into the Beijing Road + and then we take the first left and that's the first stop + the White Cloud Pagoda (*pause*) we have about half an hour or so at the pagoda + then we leave for the palace + that's down to Palace Avenue and then along (*pause*) after that we come out of the palace and go down the avenue + we go to visit the National Monument (*pause*) right + about twenty minutes there for photographs + then the bus takes us on down that road and first left to the market + and we go into the market from round the back + that's the beach side (*pause*) you'll have time to do some shopping + then back to the bus and we go along Progress Street + and the next place we visit is the Nations Museum + you'll have plenty of time for a good look round and I'll be doing a guided walk for those who want it (*pause*) and then the last stop on the tour is the silk mill + that's along Progress Street and turn right (*pause*) we have about an hour's tour at the mill + then the bus brings us back to the hotel + left into Nations Road + round the corner + and we're back at the hotel (*pause*) and that's the city tour complete'

▶ TASK 84

1 Did you experience any (listening or reading) comprehension problems as you tried to mark the tour route?

2 On the Instructions tapescript, underline the points that caused difficulty. Then compare them with our intended 'problem points' in the Tai Tu Guidelines (Appendix 2).

Grading in the Map series

The three tasks in the series—Tai Tu City Tour, Marathon, and Silver Island—incorporated five types of grading:

referring expressions completeness of map
type of map number of map features
starting points and end points

The use of the first of these factors was intended to build on the design of the earlier task series, which we discussed earlier in the Diagrams section. We will briefly comment on the other four factors.

Type of map. First, we assumed that the type of map would have an effect on listening difficulty, through the amount of helpful support it offered to the listener. It seemed to us that the demands placed on the students were less if the possible direction of the next part of the route was limited. So marking a route on the Tai Tu gridiron type map (where roads meet at right-angles and divide the areas in between into regular blocks) is less complex than working with the Marathon map which has irregular intersections and shapes. In turn, following this second type of map should be simpler than dealing with the Silver Island map, which has no roads or paths marked on it, and where the listener's orientation depends on reference to natural landmarks.

Starting points and end-points. You may recall that when you did the Tai Tu task you were told (both on the map and in your task instructions) that your coach tour would begin and end at the hotel. We assumed that being given this sort of preliminary picture of the goal of a task would help listeners to visualize what was involved, and perhaps to check their progress through the task. For Map tasks 2 and 3, no such clear indication of starting-point or destination was provided; the listeners had to work out both for themselves.

Completeness of map. The Tai Tu map was complete, in the sense that all the places the tourists would be visiting were marked and named. (The way they were named or described differed from the speaker's version, as explained in our comments on the Diagram tasks.)

The Hearer's version of the Marathon map contained three items that were marked but not named. Their identity had either to be guessed from the fact that the speaker must be referring to a feature in that general area of the map, or to be agreed on in group discussion, or confirmed/clarified by the group leader.

The Silver Island recording contained references to three natural features marked but not named on the Hearers' map. To add a further degree of difficulty, two other items referred to on tape were missing from the students' map. This made it more likely that the students would have to discuss the problem and agree on some form of action to get their doubts cleared up.

Number of map features. As in earlier series, we assumed that the scale of a comprehension task increases with the number of items referred to by a speaker which are essential to the solving of the problem. This aspect of grading was built into the three Map tasks: Tai Tu involved a total of six items, the Marathon route used ten orientation points, and there were fifteen landmarks mentioned in the Silver Island instructions.

Summary. The five factors of grading built into the Map series can be represented in Table 3.

	Grading factors				
Task no. and title	*Type of map*	*Complete-ness*	*Start/ end given?*	*Number of features*	*Referring expressions*
1 Tai Tu City Tour	gridiron; roads marked	full	yes	6	identical 1 synonymous 3 compatible 2
2 Marathon	irregular; paths marked	full	no	10	blank 2 identical 4 synonymous 3 contradictory 1
3 Silver Island	natural; landmarks	3 items missing	no	15	identical 6 synonymous 2 compatible 4 contradictory 3

Table 3: Grading in the Map series

Listeners' performances on the Map tasks
Although we were interested to observe the way in which our materials elicited a range of more or less effective listening skills from different individuals, our major concern was whether tasks like these were useful in helping them to *develop* more effective listening strategies. So we studied how the performances of each group compared when tackling different tasks over a period of two to four weeks. As in the case of the Diagram materials, we will illustrate some of the classroom performances on these Map tasks.

► TASK 85

The two extracts below are taken from recordings of the same L1 group. In the first extract, they are tackling the Diagram 2 material; in the second, they are working on the Tai Tu task. As you read the extracts, analyse what sort of skills they deploy.

Group A (Diagram 2)
Tp: 'then up at the top again in the 12% one you put "have stopped smoking" and in the other two you put "do not smoke" and "over 30 per day" '
Ps: what have you put in the 'not smoking'? / the 30% / stop it Miss what one do you put?

Group A (Map 1)
Tp: '. . . and you go into the market from round the back'
P: oh aye
Te: sure?
Ps: hmhm / there's two markets
Te: right Agnes there's two markets
Ps: where? / so what one?
Te: it's the fish market you've got to go to
Ps: what one is the fish market? / it'll be the nearest one to the sea so that'll be right—still on the right?

The diagram task was from the second set of materials these pupils attempted; the Tai Tu map task was from the third. Do you notice any signs of improvement? In which skill areas?

In the example above, an initially less successful group—also categorized by their school as of low academic ability—improve their performance with experience. In later tasks these pupils demonstrate an ability to discuss problems and solutions purposefully, and use their general knowledge to support their listening, a skill which we observed in early task performances only among more successful groups, who were also considerably more academically able than Group A.

With the L2 students we were interested to observe their positive comments, made during and after performances, on the usefulness of the types of task they were being asked to tackle. (Incidentally, we were not present, so we may assume that the comments were not made for our benefit.)

► TASK 86

Below is an extract from the Tai Tu map task. Before reading further, look at the Hearer's and Speaker's maps (Task 85 and Appendix 2) and compare the way the pagodas are marked.

1 Which student (O or Z) understands the purpose of the listening task better?

Tp: '. . . we turn into Beijing Road + and then take the first left and that's the first stop + the White Cloud Pagoda'

Z: sorry + is this some information? + is this explain? + only a name not pagoda + but it is not enough to directly explain direction + is the man enter uh go out of hotels + it is not enough + explain + + I think it must explain the go out the hotel and turn the right + cross road and then palace behind you

O: if he do that

Z: and then

O: it will be clear

Z: Beijing Road + in Beijing Road you turn on the right

O: if he do that [Z] excuse me + if you do that + why you need to listen and make it + it's clear + everybody know it

Z: yes yes you are right

O: that is this exercise + try to think which one

2 What is student Z's objection?

3 From your experience, is it usual for a student to explain the purpose of a classroom exercise, as O does?

4 Would it have been better if the teacher had given student Z the explanation, rather than leaving it to O?

It was our intention to make the teacher's role in the use of our materials one of stage manager, rather than director or leading actor. In the teacher's notes we stressed that she should as far as possible respond to the group's decisions, rather than taking the initiative in suggesting routes to solutions. She was also intended to be a source of supplementary information, if the learners found it necessary to request it. From this point of view, we judged success of the materials partly in terms of how much purposeful discussion took place among listeners, rather than between individual learner and teacher.

▶ TASK 87

Here are two extracts from performances by the same L2 class (the intermediate group). The first comes from work on the first task series they used; the second from their third.

Group H (Town Centre)

Te: tell me again [A] what you want to know

A: which corner does she speak about? + she told us a Wimpy Bar in the corner + we need to know in which street + in which corner

G: or the name of the shop + yes

B: Thomson's bakery
Te: the name of the shop? + I don't understand
A: the shop who has now became Wimpy Bar
Te: she said that + she said McPherson's
G: in?
Te: McPherson's
G: we must know the kind of shop
Te: McPherson's + you want information about McPherson's then?
Ss: yes
Te: right + and you want to know what kind of shop McPherson's is? + do you agree?
Ss: yes
Te: it's a chemist's shop

Group H (Tai Tu)
Tp: '. . . the silk mill (*shown as one of two factories on Hearer's map*) + that's along Progress Street and turn right'
Ss: stop
F: where is silk mill?
B: silk factory?
A: silk factory?
B: maybe the factory + at the left side + in the middle
F: go back?
A: oh no + she told to turn + they turn the first on the right
S: on the right + yeah
C: the right?
A: yes so if you come
S: but this factory is to the left + the factory
A: no when you come back from the museum + it's the first on the right
F: go back?
J: they turn back?
A: I think they return and turn + but I'm not sure . . .
F: why don't we ask a question?
S: yes
Te: what's your question?
F: is it the factory on Progress Street?
Te: yes

Compare the earlier and later extracts by the group. Can you identify differences between the two performances in terms of

1 the effectiveness of discussion between students
2 the precision of clarification questions
3 the role of the teacher (initiation versus response)?

We believe that the materials were useful for the L2 learners in our study.

The foreign listeners—like the native pupils—displayed a range of listening skills over the tasks. The students themselves seemed to see benefits in practising with the materials; even group G, linguistically the least proficient class, who experienced most difficulty in tackling the tasks, wanted to do more work of this type as they said they felt they were learning from it.

When asked to specify *what* they thought they had learned, group H mentioned a range of the features of listening which their experience of working on the tasks had made them aware of:

1 the need to cope with alternative descriptions of the same thing, rather than always expecting a single term

2 the way in which one small piece of language can affect the interpretation of a text

3 that some native speakers (i.e. not only these materials!) are hard to understand, making it necessary to ask for something to be clarified or repeated.

The approach we adopted in these listening materials focuses on the practice and development of the *skills of listening*. Many language teachers—and, as we saw in 5 and 6, some course writers—have tended to see listening primarily as a *language* skill. They might be surprised that we have not discussed our L2 students' problems with the language of the input materials, e.g. vocabulary and syntax, particularly as one of our groups was only at post-elementary level and the materials were not in any way adapted.

The principal reason for not mentioning language problems is quite simple: the students had fewer difficulties in these areas than one might have expected. The task procedure probably helped, since the listeners had the option of group discussion, and also unlimited opportunity to have the cassette replayed and to ask relevant questions when necessary. A final extract from a recording of the post-elementary group illustrates how a 'vocabulary problem' (in language teachers' terms) gets solved through the task procedure.

▶ TASK 88

Group G are working on the Tai Tu map task. Read through the extract carefully and identify the different types of problems revealed by individual students' comments.

Tp: '. . . the last stop on the tour is the silk mill'
Ss: silk mill?
O: + + it is the tower or . . .?
Y: it's better to + uh + we need more information
O: the silk mill in the tower or not?

Te: do you know the meaning of mill?
K: milk?
I: mill
M: mill? + it's the postman
Y: mail
Te: yes that's one kind
I: air or wind mill
Te: but this mill is for making silk + do you know silk? + + cloth
Y: it's cloth
Te: a kind of cloth
M: yeah + + elegant
K: can you write?
Te: silk mill (writes on board)
M: ah I think he go to the factory
Y: to factory but which factory
O: you have two factory
Z: yes near factory is there
Y: if we go on maybe we will know

1 What examples can you find of:
– language problems
– listening problems?

2 Which students appear to know the word 'silk'?

3 Which students are—or believe they are—familiar with the word 'mill'?

4 How well do you think this group of (post-elementary) learners cope with the problems they experience?

We think this is an interesting example, because it shows that although the input material included unfamiliar vocabulary—'silk mill'—it was the teacher and not the listeners who first raised vocabulary as a potential problem ('Do you know the meaning of mill?'). The students were attempting to solve the current part of their task, namely, to locate the position of the silk mill on their map.

Even when the problematic item had been explained by the teacher, the listening problem remained. The students (we assume) now all knew the meaning of 'silk mill', but they continued to direct their efforts to discovering how that term might relate to the information shown on their map. They decided correctly that one of the two factories was the likely destination and that asking the teacher to play the subsequent directions ('if we go on maybe we will know') would allow them to decide which factory the speaker intended to refer to. They seemed to be aware of the fact that language problems and listening problems can occur together, but that listening is not simply a question of knowing all the words in a message.

7.5 Narratives

There were four items in this series: (1) 'Border Incident', (2) 'The Purse', (3) 'The Arrest', and (4) 'The Hungarians'. The Narrative texts differed from those in the earlier series in two important ways: firstly, they were of the dynamic language type, rather than the static type (see **4.3**); secondly, the recordings were spontaneous and not scripted. In the earlier series such as Diagrams and Maps, the texts were scripted to include the 'problem points' that would provoke uncertainty and discussion. In designing the Narrative tasks, the grading factors that we took account of were those that occurred naturally in what our recorded speakers said.

▶ ## TASK 89

What would you say are the arguments for and against using spontaneous and unrehearsed stories, rather than writing a complete script or allowing the speaker to practise before the recording? (Assume that technical quality is not a problem.)

The basic procedure involved the group listening to a person describing something that had happened to them. As they listened to each narrative, the students worked with a set of pictures, in a variety of ways. The visual information was designed to support their understanding of each story.

Grading
We applied three principal grading factors in ordering the sequence of use of our recordings and in designing the support materials. These were: (1) the *scope of the task*, involving the number of important items referred to by the speaker and the degree of required reorganization of the support material; (2) the *information sequence* in the narrative, and (3) the students' likely *familiarity with the topic* of the story.

Scope of the task. Firstly, as in earlier series, we took into account the number of items mentioned by the speaker that were important to the development of their story. In this context, the term 'items' covers not only objects but also people, actions, and locations in the narratives. Any increase in the overall total tends to make the comprehension task more complex.

Secondly, although the amount of support material was the same for all four narratives (eight pictures for each task), the students were required to do more interpretative work as the series progressed.

▶ ## TASK 90

Here is a list of four alternative exercises, combining the listeners' use of a recorded text and a set of accompanying pictures. In general terms—without considering the specific details of the story—how would you order them from least difficult to most difficult? Assume that there are eight pictures for each task.

A: ordering a set of jumbled pictures
B: choosing from pairs of alternative pictures arranged in narrative order
C: describing a missing picture from an ordered series
D: selecting four relevant pictures from a jumbled set of eight

In our Narrative series, the sequence of tasks was (1) task type B, (2) type C, (3 and 4) type A. In the case of Narratives 3 and 4, the students were asked to spend some time looking at the pictures before listening to the cassette, and discussing what they thought might be a reasonable interpretation of what the story was about, and what might be an appropriate sequence of pictures to match their own version of the story. The subsequent listening task was to follow the narrative and to number their pictures to fit that story. The relative difficulty of Narrative 4 (compared to Narrative 3) was connected with our third main grading variable, familiarity of topic, which we deal with shortly.

Information sequence. In **4** we referred to research evidence that it is easier for listeners to understand a series of events described in the sequence in which they occurred than when those events are told out of order. We therefore used the relationship between the order in which events happened and the order in which the narrator told them as a grading factor in the Narrative task series.

Narrative 1 was told in chronological order; Narratives 2–4 contained deviations from natural time order. Details of the differences between their sequence of occurrence and that of the narrative are given below in the grading summary (Table 4).

One point here may be of special importance for teachers wishing to design listening comprehension activities involving recorded stories along the lines we are proposing. As we have said, our narratives were not scripted; they were told spontaneously by speakers who had been shown a selection of prompt words (e.g. 'keys', 'passport', 'station') and asked to recall any incidents that had happened to them involving one of the items in the list.

So our analysis of the event-order of the stories was carried out *after* we had collected the recordings. The narratives were not engineered to fit in with predetermined event-orders that we wanted to use; the degree of comprehension difficulty they cause listeners is a natural consequence of the way the speakers happened to tell their anecdotes. We will be returning to this point in Section Three.

Familiarity of topic. Our use of this third main grading factor was based on the available evidence from 'script' research (discussed in **1.4**). Even without having seen the sets of accompanying picture material and without having heard the four speakers' stories, you have probably already started using the titles of the four narratives as clues to their content.

▶ TASK 91

Here the titles again:

Narrative 1: 'Border Incident'
Narrative 2: 'The Purse'
Narrative 3: 'The Arrest'
Narrative 4: 'The Hungarians'

1 What 'script' do you find yourself following for each story? (This might include possible actors, actions, locations, sequences.)
2 Do any of those four titles enable you to create a clearer or more complete script than others?
3 If you wanted to order the listening texts on the basis of *title alone* (i.e. without considering text factors), how would you order them from 'least helpful' to 'most helpful'?

'The Hungarians' was used as the last text in the Narrative series, because of the likely unfamiliarity of the topic for the Scottish secondary pupils we were working with. The titles of the first three narratives could all be said to be fairly common. If you asked a group of ten people to do Task 91, the chances are that they would not invent ten totally different stories for Narratives 1–3. The sort of things that tend to happen at borders, or to purses, or in arrests, are rather limited.

However, even when we have the visual material available in front of us, the title 'The Hungarians' helps us far less. We are left with questions rather than answers. Who are the Hungarians? Where are they going? Why?

▶ TASK 92

Look at the picture set for 'The Hungarians'. *Please do not read the tapescript yet.*

1 Does the set of pictures confirm the script you predicted in Task 91?
2 What do you think is the most likely sequence of events?
3 What would a suitable story-line be to match your ordering?

When you have worked out your own narrative and picture sequence, compare your version with the tapescript. (Note that there are differences between the *chronological* order of events and the *narrative* sequence in which the speaker mentions them.)

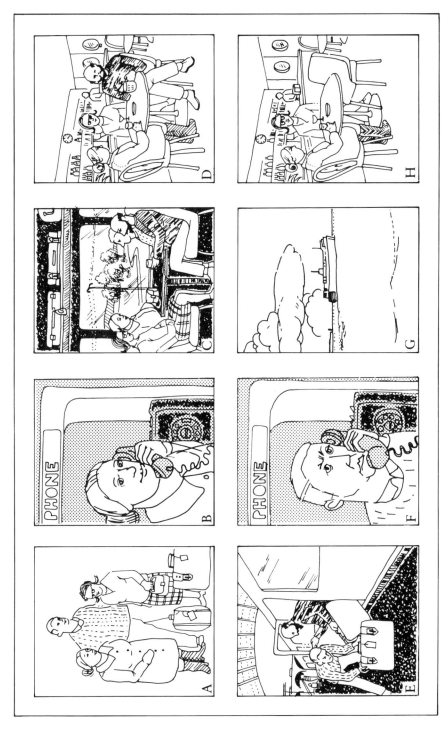

The Hungarians

Narrative 4: The Hungarians (tapescript)
'um I was once on a train from Dover to London and um + there
were three people in the compartment + there were two middle-
aged women and a middle-aged man + and they were talking away
in a language that I couldn't understand but I assumed it was an
Eastern European language + and I had seen these three on the boat
+ in the bar + and the two women were sitting at a table + and I got
the impression that the man didn't know them from before +
because he came over to their table and he seemed to be introducing
himself

anyway in the compartment they were talking and after about half
an hour or so + they stopped and I think one of them went to sleep +
and then the man started talking to me + and he'd been born in
London but his parents had come from Hungary + so he'd been
talking to the women in Hungarian + and he told me that he'd met
these two and they were coming to stay with a friend of theirs

anyway we got to Victoria Station + and he asked me to help them
with their luggage which was very heavy + so we got it all to the
platform + and then uh + he said he was going to get a trolley + and
asked if I'd wait with these two because they spoke no English + and
they'd obviously be very worried if he left them + + so off he went +
and I was standing with the two of them + and five minutes went by
+ + ten minutes went by + and eventually I realized he wasn't going
to come back

so I didn't know what to do + uh all I knew was that they had a
friend in London + so um I suppose I gestured to them to come with
me and we went up to the end of the platform to the telephones +
and they gave me a number and a name + which looked like
Elisabeth + so I rang this number + and a woman answered and I
said + 'is your name Elisveta?' or whatever it was they'd given me +
and she had a foreign accent and she said + 'my name's Elisabeth' +
+ so I said + 'ah well you don't know me + but are you expecting
two friends?' + and she said + 'no no um I don't know anybody' +
and put the phone down

so then I didn't know what to do because + I was sure I'd dialled the
right number + and I was sure that she was the woman + but I
couldn't understand why she'd hung up + so I rang again + but this
time I got one of the women to come into the phone box + and I
dialled again + and when she answered + I handed the phone to the
woman + and she started talking in Hungarian + and obviously it
had been their friend + so at that point I left them + but I still don't
know why the woman didn't admit who she was in the first
place . . .'

Solutions *Chronological sequence:* G—H—D—C—E—A—F—B
Narrative sequence: C—G—H—D—E—A—F—B

Summary The factors of grading used in the Narrative series are shown in Table 4.

Narrative	Grading factors			
	Scope of task	*Time order of story*	*Time order of pictures*	*Topic/title familiarity*
1 'Border Incident'	select	natural order	natural order	high
2 'The Purse'	follow; complete	3–4–5–7 8–6–1–2	natural order	high
3 'The Arrest'	predict; rearrange	4–1–5–6 7–8–2–3	5–7–4–8 3–2–1–6	high
4 'The Hungarians'	predict; rearrange	6–8–1–4 5–7–2–3	6–8–4–3 5–7–1–2	low

Table 4: Grading in the Narrative series

7.6 Conclusion

We have tried to give you an overall impression of the grading approach adopted in our listening development programme. You have had the chance to experience some of the comprehension texts and tasks at first hand, to analyse listeners' classroom performances, and to evaluate the extent to which listeners improved in their ability to cope with the comprehension problems the tasks were intended to set.

The principal advantage we see in this sort of graded approach is that it provides the teacher with the tools to adjust classroom activities to the level required by her students. If she knows the specific points of likely complexity in a particular text/task, she is in a position to:

– assess the listeners' performance on those points
– select or design further activities of similar, or lesser, or greater difficulty, depending on the students' ability to deal with the problems they faced
– compare performances on different task types, or on a sequence of similar tasks, and so to measure any improvement in performance.

The specific design of our materials and tasks enabled us to see that, to varying degrees, both L1 and L2 listeners became more competent at exploiting a wide range of information sources and more aware of a number of strategies that they could apply in carrying out the tasks. These include the following: (1) asking to hear the message again; (2) using relevant knowledge of the world and (3) exploiting knowledge of particular types of discourse and their linguistic conventions; (4) referring to information presented earlier in the text; (5) asking for additional information, and (6) checking with the teacher that their assumptions are correct.

We have presented excerpts from classroom transcripts because they seem to us the best way to show how listeners cope with the *process* of listening. Checking students' answer sheets after an activity is over tells us only what the result, or *product* of listening was. By encouraging and recording learner participation and discussion, we are in a better position to analyse and evaluate what individuals did to reach their solution. In Section Three we will ask you to apply this method in the evaluation of materials, tasks, and listener performances in your own classroom.

Exploration

8 Investigating listening in your classroom

The heading we have given this final section should be self-explanatory. Here the focus moves from what researchers and course writers have done on behalf of teachers to what teachers can do for *themselves*. The twenty tasks that make up the section are intended to allow you to assess the value of some theoretical issues and grading principles for work with your own students. They provide guidelines for you to explore the crucial interaction between materials and learner, between theory and informed practice.

Although you are of course free to do the tasks in any order, the sequence of presentation roughly matches that in which the relevant issues were raised in Sections One and Two. Where we think it helpful, we have made explicit references to earlier discussion.

Each task leads you to evaluate what you have just done. Your initial response to an evaluation question that asks 'Is this relevant . . .?', or 'Is this feasible', may be 'No'. But we hope that reading this book will lead you to look beyond yes/no answers, to think 'It doesn't work in my situation because . . .', or 'I could make it work with my students if I . . .'.

To adopt a culinary analogy, our aim has been to encourage teachers to be less dependent on the recipes offered by commercial materials and more aware of the essential ingredients that might make up a healthy diet of listening.

► TASK 93

Aim
To demonstrate the interdependence of speaking and listening skills.

Resources
A cassette recorder. Two versions of a simple map, with a key item marked on one but not the other. For example, it could be an island map with a route to buried treasure. The second copy of the map should be similar but not identical; of course, it must not show the route, but there might also be features missing or shown with an alternative label. (The number and type of these mismatches is one way of grading a series of tasks: see Table 3 in 7.4 for suggestions.)

Procedure
Choose two of the more confident students to demonstrate the task. Sit them opposite each other with a file or book propped up between them, to

prevent them seeing each other's paper. Give partner **A** the map with the route marked on it and partner **B** the one without. Explain that the maps were drawn by different explorers and may differ in some details. Ask **A** to tell **B** where to draw in the route to the treasure. Emphasize that it is important for **B** to ask questions if difficulties arise.

Record the performance and allow the other students to observe.

Evaluation
At the end of the task, compare maps. Replay the cassette and ask the participants first how they feel they coped. Then ask the observing students to comment on the two partners' performance. Point out any additional features that the class has not noticed.

(In **2** we saw that **B** partners typically do not challenge instructions sufficiently: they allow too many ambiguities to pass by; they fail to explain how their map differs from partner **A**'s version. Similarly, **A** partners are often so concerned with giving the instructions that they do not respond adequately to comments from **B**).

Point out that being a good listener in this sort of situation involves *speaking*, asking the right sort of questions at the right time: being a good speaker means *listening* and responding to your partner.

Get the class to complete a similar task in pairs.

▶ TASK 94

Aim
To demonstrate the particular importance for L2 speakers of indicating when they do not understand.

Resources
Copies of Task 36 dialogue.

Procedure
Ask the students to read through the dialogue between the student (NNS) and the typist (NS), and to answer these questions:

1 How many times did NNS not understand what NS said?

2 How did she indicate that she had not understood?

3 How did she manage to keep the conversation going?

Describe the three listener skills listed after Task 36 and ask the students to find examples in the dialogue. Suggest alternative expressions which can be used to signal a failure to understand (e.g. 'Sorry?' for 'Pardon me?').

Get them to act out the dialogue in pairs.

Evaluation
How well do the students think the NNS coped? Do they think she managed to get her thesis typed?

▶ TASK 95

Aim
To provide practice in applying the listening strategies from Task 94.

Resources
A cassette recorder. Role-play instructions for small tasks that students must achieve by engaging a NS (you) in conversation. For example, they might be asked to find out from you how to phone home from Britain. (Make sure you design tasks that you have answers to!)

Procedure
Act out the role-plays, with you as the NS and students as NNSs. Express parts of the information in a way that will cause the listener some difficulty—e.g. by using unfamiliar vocabulary—to give the listener a communicative need to ask for repetition, clarification, etc. Record the series of interactions.

Evaluation
Listen to the recordings one at a time. First, give the listener a chance to say how they would say things differently if they had a second chance. Then ask the other students to comment on how well the listener dealt with comprehension problems by questioning and signalling difficulties to the NS.

▶ TASK 96

Aim
To compare the relative difficulty of summary and recall tasks for L2 listeners. (See **2.5** for the problems that teenage L1 listeners had in switching listening purpose.)

Resources
Task 51 and your response to it. A short factual passage recorded on cassette. Cassette recorder.

Procedure
1 Ask your students to listen to the cassette once and then to write down as much as possible of the content, as if for someone who has not heard it. They may write in their L1, if you are able to read it. Collect in what they have written.

2 For the second hearing, ask the students to write a short summary of the text. Play the cassette straight through. It is very important that they should not have access to what they wrote at stage 1. Collect in their summaries.

Evaluation
Read the two pieces of writing produced by each individual. Are there differences between the two answers? The tendency we observed in L1 teenagers was for them to write as much, if not more, in the 'summary' as in

the first recall task. Do your students seem better able than those L1 listeners to distinguish between the different purposes? If so, what might be the positive influences on your students' performances?

▶ TASK 97

Aim
To see if grading by topic knowledge would be different from grading by student interest. (In **2** we referred to research evidence that the former may be more helpful than the latter.)

Resources
A listening course that defines its contents in terms of clear topical headings. If you have none available, you can use this list (adapted from O'Neill and Scott 1974):

industrial relations	magistrates' courts
war	special education
police	feminism
football	race relations
social work	automation

(All offer a British perspective on the issue in question.)

Procedure
Ask the students to put the topics you give them into two sequences:

A in order of how much they think they know about them
B in order of how interesting they find them.

Evaluation
How similar are individual learners' two sequences? How much agreement do you find among the (A) and (B) sequences of different students?

If you find that there is great variation, what seem to be the reasons for the differences in level of knowledge or interest? Is there sufficient consensus among your students to base the ordering of units in a programme of listening activities on either their topic knowledge or their level of interest?

▶ TASK 98

Aim
To assess the importance of using factual as well as linguistic knowledge when listening.

Resources
Prepare three short talks on how to do/make something (e.g. making an omelette, changing a tyre, growing tomatoes). Write two questions for each talk, with alternative answers provided.

Procedure

1 Give the students the questions for the first talk, telling them to choose their answers while they listen. Give the first talk.

2 Before the second talk, discuss the general topic of the talk with the class; do this in their L1 if possible, but in English if it is a mixed-language class. Do not deal with the specific content of the talk, but with the general area; for example, in the case of growing tomatoes, you might discuss why people grow vegetables and which ones they choose to grow. Then give the second talk, with students answering their questions as you are speaking.

3 Before the third talk, give the students the title of the talk and allow them to conduct their own pre-listening activities.

Evaluation
Discuss the three activities with the students. Which did they find easiest? Why?

Do their impressions actually match our discussion (see **2.3** and **2.4**) of the helpful effect of using factual background knowledge when listening?

If their order of difficulty of the three talks is different to what you expected, is it because they already knew more about one talk topic than the others? If so, that would still suggest that listeners benefit from using what they know.

▶ TASK 99

Aim
To investigate ways of encouraging listeners to use their factual knowledge in listening.

Resources
Two classes of students at similar L2 level, or two groups from the same class. Pie-chart materials: hearer's initial version and instructions from Task 78; speaker's guidelines from Appendix 1. Paper and pencils for students. A cassette recorder.

Procedure
Try out the pie-chart task, recording the performances. If you think that the smoking data in the pie-chart is reasonably similar to the smoking habits in the country where you teach, you could replace 'Scotland' in our material with the name of that country. This would make it possible for your students to use their own background knowledge. Read the tapescript, with pauses as indicated. The students can ask you to re-read any part of the instructions or to answer any question if a problem occurs.

With one group, answer each individual student's question, using the guidelines shown in Appendix 1.

With the other group, encourage the students to discuss individuals' questions before you answer them. You might say something on these lines: 'That's a good question, but I want you to talk about it with the others first.

See if anyone has any ideas about possible answers, from what they know or from what they've heard. When you've done that, I'll give you more information if you still think you need it.'

You can adapt this approach as the task progresses, but refer all questions back for discussion by the group, for them to attempt to solve the problem by pooling their knowledge.

Evaluation

1 At the end of both sessions, invite comments from the students on whether they felt such listening exercises were useful. If so, what exactly do they think they have learnt? Can you identify any difference between the responses of the students following the 'individual' and 'group' approaches?

2 Listen carefully to the recordings of the two groups. How well does each group perform? What are the differences between them? Are the questions 'better' in one group?

3 What modifications to the materials or the procedure would you make to encourage listeners to use a wide range of information sources—e.g. knowledge of pie-charts, of smoking habits, of the language—to support their listening?

▶ TASK 100

Aim
To examine the contribution of students' and teacher's talk in listening work and its possible use in assessing students' progress.

Resources
Your teaching experience and the Diagram and Map tasks in 7.

Procedure
Imagine you have been trying out the Diagram and Map materials, which are designed to encourage learners to intervene for clarification and to discuss problems. You have used them with three EFL classes—post-elementary Group A, intermediate Group B, and advanced Group C. You have recorded the students working in groups on the tasks over a period of two to three weeks and from listening to the cassettes you have calculated how much of the discussion is teacher talk and how much is student talk. The results—which are in fact figures from our own classroom study—are shown in Table 5.

	Group A		Group B		Group C	
	% T talk	% S talk	% T talk	% S talk	% T talk	% S talk
Task set 1	37	63	33	67	7	93
Task set 2	15	85	14	86	11	89
Task set 3	15	85	18	82	4	96

Table 5: Proportion of teacher talk and student talk, by task

Evaluation

1 What do these figures suggest about who is responsible for most of the problem-solving discussion arising from the listening tasks?
2 Is the pattern the same for groups at different L2 levels?
3 What do you notice as the groups progress through the tasks?
4 Is this data useful in evaluating the listening materials? If so, which aspect of the materials does it illuminate?

▶ TASK 101

Aim
To give listeners practice in coping with material containing a range of referring expressions.

Resources
Tai Tu map task (Task 83). Copies of the hearer's map for your students. Cassette recorder to record class interaction.

Procedure
In order to familiarize the students with the visual material before listening, ask them to decide which four Tai Tu sights they would choose to visit on a day's tour.

Read the introduction (after Task 83) and the instructions tapescript, making pauses where indicated. Let the students ask for repetition or clarification when in difficulty, and discuss their problems with their classmates.

Evaluation

1 Play back the recording to the students. Note where comprehension problems arose.
2 Ask the students to discuss why those difficulties came up and how well they coped with them.
3 You may find it helpful to match your students' problems with the ones built into the Tai Tu task design (Table 3 in 7.4). In particular, see whether the referring expressions led to requests for repetition and clarification. If not, ask the students how they were able to deal with the potentially conflicting information.
4 Invite students' comments on the usefulness of this specific sort of task. Were they aware before of the problems of alternative referring expressions?

▶ TASK 102

Aim
To compare the characteristics of a listening text with the focus of the listening tasks.

Resources

A set of listening materials which you have not used yourself. Cassette and recorder.

Procedure

1 Select a listening text and play the cassette once straight through. Do not look at either the students' tasks or the tapescript. As you listen, make a brief note of the key points in what the speaker says and any impressions about the way he or she talks to the listener.

2 Now read through the tasks in the student's book. Are you able to answer them after one hearing?

Evaluation

1 Compare the notes you made with the points selected by the course writer. To what extent do they match? Has the writer included points that you have left out, or vice versa? Have you made any note of the relationship between speaker and listener? Do any of the questions direct learners' attention to that relationship?

2 Which do you think reflect the original text better: your notes or the official questions? Why?

3 Do any of the writer's questions change (i.e. exaggerate or reduce) the importance of points in the text?

▶ **TASK 103**

Aim

To investigate the effects of the 'teaching' or 'testing' orientation of a listening task.

Resources

Task 56 and your response to it. A cassette recorder. If possible, use the original listening material for Exercise B in Task 56 (Underwood and Barr 1980). If not, take any exercise from material you know where the learners are asked to listen for and identify a number of items, actions, events, etc.

Procedure

1 Ask half the class to discuss possible items (etc.) that they think might be mentioned, given what they know about the speaker, the context, and so on. They should draw up a checklist of the various possibilities that emerge in their discussion.

2 Do not allow the other students to observe or take part in the discussion, or to see the checklist.

3 Play the cassette. The two groups answer their own type of question: the discussion group tick items on their list; the second group write down the points as they hear them.

Evaluation

Do differences emerge between the two groups? Firstly, ask the students themselves to say how easy or difficult they found the task. (This can be done quickly by asking them to rate it on a scale from 1–6, easy to difficult.)

Secondly, collect in their written answers and compare them. Can you see any difference in quality/quantity/accuracy of the answers produced by the pre-listeners who received the 'teaching' oriented task, and the others who were simply tested on their listening?

▶ ## TASK 104

Aim

To compare learners' and course writers' perceptions of listening difficulty.

Resources

Two listening activities of a similar type, if possible from a course that makes its grading explicit—e.g. *Task Listening* (Blundell and Stokes 1981). The two activities selected should come from early and late in the course sequence; that is, they should be relatively easy and relatively difficult, according to the course writer(s).

Procedure

Complete the two listening activities according to the teacher's notes. Play the more difficult text first, but do not tell your students that you are changing the intended order.

Evaluation

1 Ask the students to say which exercise they found easier and why. Make a careful note of the factors they perceived as different in the two activities. (If possible, record the post-listening discussion.)

2 Analyse their perceptions of complexity and compare them with those that feature in the course writer's grading description.

3 Do you find that in fact your students expressed common types of difficulty, or were their comments highly individual ones? Can they be accounted for in terms of the 'control panel' analogy (Figure 6 in **6.4**)?

▶ ## TASK 105

Aim

To examine ways of reducing listening difficulty by adjustments to text or task.

Resources

The text below. Although invented, it approximates to what a real-life listening input might be like. To make it easier to read quickly, it has been written in sentences. In actual speech the moves from one utterance to the next would be less clear-cut than in the printed form.

Procedure
Read it through, monitoring any difficulties in comprehension as you do so.

> 'The first person you'll come across is the receptionist. She isn't medically trained, so there's no point in telling her all the symptoms. Either make an appointment or explain that it's urgent and you need to see someone about the baby. The rule there is that if they wear ordinary clothes, they're not medically qualified. Doctors wear white coats, nurses wear white dresses, health visitors have blue ones. You can go every week to get the baby weighed, or to ask about feeding or anything. You don't need an appointment because that's the health visitors, I think, anyway they wear blue dresses. They tell you when to make an appointment with the doctor for jabs and things. Oh, and they do the baby's check-ups, too, to see she's developing OK, and eye and hearing tests as well. Yes, all the routine checks are the health visitors. They're there every afternoon. If she's not well, though, it's the doctor. She's very nice and she'll give you a prescription for medicine or whatever. So that's it really, that's who's at the clinic to look after the baby. The receptionist makes the appointments, the health visitors do all the routine checks, and the doctor sees you by appointment if the baby's ill.'

Evaluation

1 Would the text be (relatively speaking) easy or difficult for an intermediate-level L2 listener?

2 How might you make the *text* less demanding? You could consider at least the following possibilities: editing; rearranging; altering.

3 What else might you do to make listening to such material easier, *without changing the text*?

► TASK 106

Aim
To try out alternative versions of the same listening task.

Resources
Two sets of material based on the Health Centre text (Task 105); two classes at similar levels; a cassette recorder.

Procedure
Run one version of the Health Centre task with each group. Record their performances.

Evaluation

1 Ask the students to comment on the ease or difficulty of their exercise.

2 Ask them to specify what made it easy or difficult.

3 Compare the two classes by:

- listening to the recorded interaction during the task
- listening to their post-listening discussion
- analysing their written task answers.

4 Does one version emerge as easier? If so, is it the one you designed to be easier? Or is the evidence unclear?

5 Arrange a follow-up task with the same groups that will enable you to get a clearer answer to Evaluation point 4.

▶ # TASK 107

Aim
This task is linked with Task 108. They are intended to allow you to examine the basis for an author's claim to have graded listening activities in a course.

Resources
The introduction (probably in the Teacher's Book) to a course that is explicitly graded, i.e. one that includes an explanation of the grading factors used in its design.

Procedure
Read the description carefully. Note down the factors that have been taken into account in grading the units.

Evaluation
1 Can you match those grading factors against our summary lists of *input* features (end of **6.2**) and of *content/task* features (end of **6.3**)? Are other factors incorporated in the course's grading scheme? If so, does their inclusion seem reasonable?

2 Can you identify factors that could be used to establish an *alternative* sequence of units to that offered by the course writer(s)? Write out your own order of unit numbers.

▶ # TASK 108

Aim
To try out an alternative ordering of published listening materials.

Resources
Your re-ordered list of units from Task 107. The relevant cassette and print material.

Procedure
1 Select three units from early, middle, and late in your own sequence.
2 Use the units (either in a single lesson or a series of lessons), following the course instructions.

Evaluation
1 Ask the students to say which exercise they found easiest and why. Make

a careful note of the factors they perceived as different in the three units. (If possible, record the post-listening discussion.)

2 Analyse their perceptions of complexity against those that you used to re-order the course units, and those featured in the course writer's grading description.

3 As in Task 104, do you find that the students perceived common types of difficulty, or were their problems specific to individuals?

▶ TASK 109

Aim
To complete the design of a graded set of listening tasks targeted on the listening problems of a particular group of students.

Resources
The results of Task 101; the map grading summary in Table 3.

Procedure
Use the results of your students' discussion in Task 101 to design further listening tasks based on maps; adapt the Table 3 guidelines according to the Task 101 results. For example, if the Tai Tu task seemed rather long and complex for your students, then the 'number of features' factor should be only slightly increased, from 6 to 7, say, rather than to 10 as in our own second map task. As far as 'referring expressions' are concerned, if the students had difficulty in dealing with *compatible* expressions in Tai Tu, then in your second task you should include items that will practise that sort of identification.

Remember to include pauses in the script you write for yourself and to indicate the 'problem points' you have designed. Draw two versions of the map: the hearer's version for the students and a speaker's version for you to refer to. (The map need not be a work of art—something simple is what is needed.)

Evaluation
Follow the evaluation process as in Task 101. Compare the results there with those you noted for your own task.

You can then design further items in the series according to your findings on the two 'pilot studies' you have carried out in the last two Tasks.

▶ TASK 110

Aim
To pilot your map materials with different groups of learners.

Resources
Materials from Task 109; two L2 classes at similar levels; cassette recorder.

Procedure
1 Use the map materials with the two groups of students. As before, you

may use the series of tasks over a number of lessons or in a single session.

2 Record the resulting classroom interaction.

3 Ask the students to comment on any difficulties they encountered.

Evaluation

1 Listen carefully to the recordings of the performances.

2 What differences do you notice between the groups? Were there points that caused problems for one group and not the other?

3 Which points did both classes find problematic?

4 What adjustments would you now make to the task procedure or materials design?

▶ ## TASK 111

Aim
To design a graded set of narrative listening materials.

Resources
A number of native speakers, preferably, or reasonably fluent L2 speakers. A list of topics, some of whose associated vocabulary is likely to be familiar to your students. A cassette recorder.

Procedure

1 Ask a number of friends or colleagues if they can recall and relate an incident that has happened to them, in relation to the topics in your list. (These can be single-word cues; the ones in our own list included 'passport', 'ticket', 'police', 'keys'. Others might be 'first trip abroad', 'my worst ever journey', 'an accident'.)

2 Record individual speakers telling their story. Collect about six anecdotes.

3 Listen carefully to the recordings. Your aim is to select and grade, say, three narratives. Some may need to be rejected because of sound quality, or because the speaker ran out of things to say, or because the story involves too much unfamiliar vocabulary.

4 Choose the criteria by which you will grade the stories for difficulty. You could refer back to Table 4 in 7.5; but you may need to take into account other grading factors when you have heard your collected stories. We suggest you include at least *time order* of the events described and also *topic familiarity* in your grading factors.

5 Decide the order of difficulty of the three narratives *in terms of your own grading criteria*.

6 Design appropriate tasks for listeners to perform as they listen. Keep in mind the relationship between task difficulty and input difficulty. You might want to use picture tasks (on the lines of Tasks 90 and 92) or you could substitute words or phrases if producing pictures is impractical.

Remember, too, that pre-listening activities are valuable in preparing students for listening (cf. Tasks 91 and 99).

Evaluation

1 Ask the students to compare their performances on the three tasks. Did they find the same problem in each narrative?

2 Do the students' answers and comments match your predictions about the likely factors of difficulty?

3 Make any adjustments you think necessary to your narrative task set, according to the results of this pilot study.

4 If possible, try out the amended set with another group of students.

▶ ## TASK 112

Aim

To evaluate the effectiveness of different listening materials and to involve learners in the evaluation process.

Resources

Two different sets of listening materials, each consisting of three tasks, either from published sources or of your own design. Two roughly comparable groups of L2 listeners. Cassette recorder to record students' comments, questions, etc.

Procedure

(This can be done over a number of lessons.) Work through the two sets of materials with the different classes, preferably using a group discussion method (as in Task 99), but at least allowing learners to stop and question at any point where they experience difficulty.

Evaluation

1 After completing the tasks, play back the cassette and ask the students to discuss/explain the reasons for the problems they encountered and, if possible, to suggest solutions.

2 Ask students to compare their performances on the first and last tasks of their set, to see if the types of difficulty they experienced were the same. Is there any evidence of improvement in listening skills?

3 Listen to the recording you have made of the classroom interaction. You will now probably notice things that you missed in the classroom. How do the recorded performances fit in with the *aims* of the material? What skills were the tasks designed to develop? How well did they succeed for your students? Were any principles of grading involved? If so, were they helpful?

4 You can then compare the results of this exercise with the two parallel groups. Does it offer you any insight into the comparative effectiveness of the materials for your students? If not, what are the factors that prevent you making that sort of comparison?

Glossary

comprehensible input: language including elements above a learner's current L2 level, but which they understand by using additional contextual or schematic information.

co-text: the other parts of a text, both preceding and following the piece of language currently being produced.

interactional talk: speech whose primary purpose is social, to establish or maintain friendly relations between interlocutors.

interactive model of speech perception: a view of speech perception that assumes we make simultaneous use of as many relevant sources of information as possible and achieve comprehension by integrating the data.

interlocutor: a participant in a conversation.

listener-friendly: expressed in such a way as to make the listener's task easy.

mental model: the listener's internal picture or representation of the message a speaker is trying to convey.

on-line comprehension: understanding something at natural speed and as it is being said, rather than after the event.

reciprocal listening: listening where there is the opportunity for the listener to take on the role of speaker.

referential communication paradigm: an experimental task requiring the listener to identify one item (from a set of similar items) being described by the speaker.

referring expression: a word or phrase used to refer to a person, object, etc. already mentioned or understood.

schema (plural **schemata**): a mental framework of knowledge and experience that allows us to incorporate what we hear into what we know.

script: a set or sequence of likely actions, events, and actors in a familiar situation, such as that of cashing a cheque in a bank.

serial bottom-up model: a (simplistic) view of comprehension that assumes we understand speech by working through a series of stages, starting with individual sounds and gradually building up to an understanding of the whole message.

systemic knowledge: a listener's knowledge of the system (phonology, grammar, and semantics) of a particular language.

top-down processing: using global expectations about what someone is about to say to help you build up your comprehension of their message.

transactional talk: communication, the main purpose of which is to achieve a successful transfer of information.

Further reading

On spoken language

Three books that cover complementary areas within the teaching of oral communication:

Brown, G., A. Anderson, R. Shillcock, and **G. Yule.** 1984. *Teaching Talk.* Cambridge: Cambridge University Press.
This offers an objective approach to the teaching and assessment of L1 speaking skills.

Brown, G. and **G. Yule.** 1983a. *Teaching the Spoken Language.* Cambridge: Cambridge University Press.
Examines the characteristics of spoken language and their implications for teaching; essentially L2-oriented.

Bygate, M. 1987. *Speaking.* Oxford: Oxford University Press.
The author emphasizes the symbiotic relationship of speaking and listening as twin L2 conversation skills.

On course materials/design

Nunan, D. 1988. *Syllabus Design.* Oxford: Oxford University Press.
This provides a comprehensive treatment of alternative approaches to syllabus design in language teaching.

Ur, P. 1984. *Teaching Listening Comprehension.* Cambridge: Cambridge University Press.
This focuses in particular on materials/activities to practise listening and offers a compendium of task types, with illustrations from published and unpublished materials.

On issues raised in this book

The following offer interesting follow-up reading on issues that we have been able only to touch on in this book:

Applied Linguistics 7/3. 1986.
This is a special issue on language comprehension. In particular, the articles by Faerch and Kasper and Sharwood Smith are interesting speculations on how listening might result in learning.

Brown, G. and **G. Yule.** 1983b. *Discourse Analysis.* Cambridge: Cambridge University Press.
Chapter 7 is a concise and non-technical review of research (from a wide range of academic fields) into listeners'/readers' use of background knowledge in achieving comprehension.

Long, M. H. 1983. 'Linguistic and conversational adjustments to non-native speakers.' *Studies in Second Language Acquisition* 5/2: 177–93.
This article summarizes research into the formal and functional modifications that are likely to be made to help L2 listeners in face-to-face conversation.

McGovern, J. (ed.) 1983. *Video Applications in Language Teaching.* Oxford: Pergamon.
An early—and still perhaps the best—collection of articles on the potential role of video in developing comprehension skills.

Winitz, H. (ed.) 1981. *The Comprehension Approach to Foreign Language Teaching.* Rowley, Mass.: Newbury House.
Contributions on Comprehension Approach techniques in a variety of contexts, including secondary school.

Bibliography

Anderson, A. H., G. Brown, and G. Yule. 1984. 'Hearer effects on speaker performances.' *First Language* 5: 23–40.

Anderson, A. H. and E. Boyle. (in progress) 'Listening skills: creating the classroom context to promote successful listening.' Scottish Education Department research report.

Asher, S. R. 1976. 'Children's ability to appraise their own and another person's communication performance.' *Developmental Psychology* 12: 24–32.

Bard, E. G. and A. H. Anderson. 1983. 'The unintelligibility of parental speech.' *Journal of Child Language* 10: 1–18.

Bartlett, F. C. 1932. *Remembering*. Cambridge: Cambridge University Press.

Benson, P. C. and C. Hjelt. 1978. 'Listening competence: a prerequisite to communication.' *Modern Language Journal* 62/1: 85–9.

Blundell, L. and J. Stokes. 1981. *Task Listening*. Cambridge: Cambridge University Press.

Bower, G., J. Black, and T. Turner. 1979. 'Scripts in memory for texts.' *Cognitive Psychology* 3: 193–209.

Brown, A., S. Smiley, J. Day, M. Townsend, and S. Lawton. 1977. 'Intrusion of a thematic idea in children's comprehension and retention of stories.' *Child Development* 48: 1454–66.

Brown, G. 1986a. 'Grading and professionalism in ELT' in P. Meara (ed.): *Spoken Language*. British Studies in Applied Linguistics 1. London: Centre for Information on Language Teaching and Research.

Brown, G. 1986b. 'Investigating listening comprehension in context.' *Applied Linguistics* 7/3: 284–302.

Brown, G., A. H. Anderson, N. Shadbolt, and A. J. Lynch. 1987. 'Listening comprehension skills in secondary pupils.' Summary of Scottish Education Department research report.

Brown, G., A. H. Anderson, R. Shillcock, and G. Yule. 1984. *Teaching Talk*. Cambridge: Cambridge University Press.

Brown, G. and G. Yule. 1983a. *Teaching the Spoken Language*. Cambridge: Cambridge University Press.

Brown, G. and G. Yule. 1983b. *Discourse Analysis*. Cambridge: Cambridge University Press.

Brown, T. and M. Hayes. 1985. 'Literacy background and reading development in a second language' in T. H. Carr (ed.): *The Development of Reading Skills*. San Francisco: Jossey-Bass.

Butterfield, E. and G. Siperstein. 1974. 'Influence of contingent auditory stimulation upon non-nutritional suckle' in *Proceedings of Third Symposium on Oral Sensation and Perception: the Mouth of the Infant*. Springfield, Ill.: Charles C. Thomas.

Butterworth, G. 1972. 'A Spanish-speaking Adolescent's Acquisition of English Syntax.' MA TESL thesis, University of California, Los Angeles.

Bygate, M. 1987. *Speaking.* In the series: *Language Teaching: a Scheme for Teacher Education.* Oxford: Oxford University Press.

Carr, T. H., T. Brown, and **C. Vavrus.** 1985. 'A component skills analysis of reading performance' in T. H. Carr (ed.): *The Development of Reading Skills.* San Francisco: Jossey-Bass.

Chaudron, C. 1983a. 'Foreigner talk in the classroom—an aid to learning?' in H. Seliger and M. H. Long (eds.): *Classroom Oriented Research in Second Language Acquisition.* Rowley, Mass.: Newbury House.

Chaudron, C. 1983b. 'Simplification of input: topic reinstatements and their effects on L2 learners' recognition and recall.' *TESOL Quarterly* 17/3: 437–58.

Chaudron, C. 1985. 'Comprehension, comprehensibility and learning in the second language classroom.' *Studies in Second Language Acquisition* 7/2: 216–32.

Cole, R. A. and **J. Jakimik.** 1978. 'Understanding speech: how words are heard' in G. Underwood (ed.): *Strategies of Information Processing.* New York: Academic Press.

Cole, R. A. and **J. Jakimik.** 1980. 'A model of speech perception' in R. A. Cole (ed.): *Perception and Production of Fluent Speech.* Hillsdale, NJ: Erlbaum.

Conrad, L. 1985. 'Semantic versus syntactic cues in listening comprehension.' *Studies in Second Language Acquisition* 7/1: 59–72.

Cook, G. (forthcoming) *Discourse.* In the series: *Language Teaching: a Scheme for Teacher Education.* Oxford: Oxford University Press.

Cook, V. J. 1973. 'The comparison of language development in native children and foreign adults.' *International Review of Applied Linguistics* 11: 13–28.

Cosgrove, J. M. and **C. J. Patterson.** 1977. 'Plans and the development of listener skills.' *Developmental Psychology* 13: 557–64.

d'Anglejan, A. and **G. R. Tucker.** 1975. 'The acquisition of complex English structures by adult learners.' *Language Learning* 5/2: 281–96.

Davies, N. F. 1978. 'Putting receptive skills first: an investigation into sequencing in modern language teaching.' Linköping, Sweden: University of Linköping.

Dittman, A. T. 1972. 'Developmental factors in conversational behaviour.' *The Journal of Communication* 22: 404–23.

Elman, J. and **J. McLelland.** 1984. 'Speech perception as a cognitive process: the interactive activitation model' in *Speech and Language: Advances in Basic Research and Practice* Volume 10. New York: Academic Press.

Ervin-Tripp, S. M. 1979. 'Children's verbal turn-taking' in E. Ochs and B. Schiefflin (eds.): *Developmental Pragmatics.* New York: Academic Press.

Faerch, C. and **G. Kasper.** 1983. 'Introduction' in C. Faerch and G. Kasper (eds.): *Strategies in Interlanguage Communication.* London: Longman.

Faerch, C. and **G. Kasper.** 1986. 'The role of comprehension in second language learning.' *Applied Linguistics* 7/3: 257–74.

Favreau, M. and **N. Segalowitz.** 1983. 'Automatic and controlled processes in the first and second language reading of fluent bilinguals.' *Memory and Cognition* 11/6: 565–74.

Ferguson, N. and **M. O'Reilly.** 1977. *Listening and Note-taking.* London: Unwin Hyman.

Gallagher, T. 1977. 'Revision behaviours in the speech of normal children developing language.' *Journal of Speech and Hearing Research* 21: 103–17.

Garrod, S. 1986. 'Language comprehension in context: a psychological perspective.' *Applied Linguistics* 7/3: 226–38.

Gass, S. and **C. Madden** (eds.). 1985. *Input in Second Language Acquisition.* Rowley, Mass.: Newbury House.

Glenn, C. 1978. 'The role of episodic structure and story length in children's recall of simple stories.' *Journal of Verbal Learning and Verbal Behaviour* 17: 229–47.

Gluckberg, S., R. M. Kraus, and **E. Higgins.** 1975. 'The development of referential communication skills' in F. D. Horowitz (ed.): *Review of Child Development Research* Volume 4. Chicago: University of Chicago Press.

Graesser, A., N. Hoffman, and **L. Clark.** 1980. 'Structural components of reading time.' *Journal of Verbal Learning and Verbal Behaviour* 19: 135–51.

Haberlandt, K. and **G. Bingham** 1984. 'The effect of input direction on the processing of script statements.' *Journal of Verbal Learning and Verbal Behaviour* 23: 162–77.

Hare, V. C. and **D. Devine.** 1983. 'Topical knowledge and topical interest as predictors of listening comprehension.' *Journal of Educational Research* 76/3: 157–60.

Hatch, E. 1978. 'Discourse analysis in second language acquisition' in E. Hatch (ed.): *Second Language Acquisition.* Rowley, Mass.: Newbury House.

Hatch, E., S. Peck, and **J. Wagner-Gough.** 1979. 'A look at process in child second language acquisition' in E. Ochs and B. Schiefflin (eds.): *Developmental Pragmatics.* New York: Academic Press.

Horgan, D. 1978. 'How to answer questions when you've got nothing to say.' *Journal of Child Language* 5: 159–65.

Hutchinson, T. and **A. Waters.** 1981. 'Performance and competence in English for Specific Purposes.' *Applied Linguistics* 2/1: 56–69.

Ironsmith, M. and **G. Whitehurst.** 1978. 'How children learn to listen: the effects of modelling feedback styles on children's performance in referential communication.' *Developmental Psychology* 14: 546–54.

James, K., R. R. Jordan, and **A. Matthews.** 1979. *Listening Comprehension and Notetaking Course.* Glasgow: Collins.

Johnson, P. 1982. 'Effects on reading comprehension of building background knowledge.' *TESOL Quarterly* 16/4: 503–16.

Johnson-Laird, P. 1980. *Mental Models.* Cambridge: Cambridge University Press.

Jordan, R. R. 1982. *Figures in Language.* Glasgow: Collins.

Kaplan, E. 1969. 'The Role of Intonation in the Acquisition of Language.' Unpublished Ph.D. thesis, Cornell University.

Kaplan, E. and **G. Kaplan.** 1970. 'The prelinguistic child' in J. Eliot (ed.): *Human Development and Cognitive Processes.* New York: Holt, Rinehart and Winston.

Kintsch, W. and **S. Young.** 1984. 'Selective recall of decision-relevant information from texts.' *Memory and Cognition* 12/2: 112–17.

Krashen, S. 1981. *Second Language Acquisition and Second Language Learning.* Oxford: Pergamon.

Lee, W. J. 1977. 'What type of syllabus for the teaching of English as a foreign or second language?' *International Review of Applied Linguistics* 15/3: 246–9.

Liberman, A. M. 1970. 'The grammars of speech and language.' *Cognitive Psychology* 1: 301–23.

Long, M. H. 1983. 'Linguistic and conversational adjustments to non-native speakers.' *Studies in Second Language Acquisition* 5/2: 177–93.

Lynch, A. J. 1984. 'Realistic texts and realistic targets in L2 listening comprehension.' Paper presented at 2nd TESOL Scotland Conference, Falkirk, Scotland, October 1984.

Lynch, A. J. 1987. 'Modifications to foreign listeners: the stories teachers tell.' ERIC Document ED 274 225. Washington: Centre for Applied Linguistics.

Lynch, A. J. 1988a.'Grading Foreign Language Listening Materials: the Use of Naturally Modified Interaction.' Ph.D. thesis, University of Edinburgh.

Lynch, A. J. 1988b. 'Speaking up or talking down?: foreign learners' reaction to teacher talk.' *English Language Teaching Journal* 42/2: 109–16.

Lynch,T. 1983. *Study Listening*. Cambridge: Cambridge University Press.

McCarthy, M. (forthcoming) *Vocabulary*. In the series: *Language Teaching: a Scheme for Teacher Education*. Oxford: Oxford University Press.

McDonough, S. 1981. *Psychology and Foreign Language Teaching*. London: George Allen and Unwin.

McGovern, J. (ed.). 1983. *Video Applications in Language Teaching*. Oxford: Pergamon.

Mackey, W. F. 1954. 'What to look for in a method: grading.' *English Language Teaching Journal* 8: 45–58.

McLean, A. 1981. *Start Listening*. London: Longman.

MacWilliam, I. 1986. 'Video and language comprehension.' *English Language Teaching Journal* 40/2: 131–35.

Markman, E. M. 1977. 'Realizing you don't understand: a preliminary investigation.' *Child Development* 48: 986–92.

Markman, E. M. 1979. 'Realizing you don't understand: elementary school children's awareness of inconsistencies'. *Child Development* 50: 643–55.

Marslen-Wilson, W. D. 1975. 'Sentence perception as an interactive parallel process.' *Science* 189: 226–8.

Marslen-Wilson, W. D. and **L. Tyler.** 1980. 'The temporal structure of spoken language understanding.' *Cognition* 8: 1–71.

Marslen-Wilson, W. D. and **A. Welsh.** 1978. 'Processing interactions and lexical access during word recognition in continuous speech.' *Cognitive Psychology* 10: 29–63.

Mueller, G. A. 1980. 'Visual contextual clues and listening comprehension: an experiment.' *Modern Language Journal* 64/3: 335–40.

Nakazima, S. 1962. 'A comparative study of the speech development of Japanese and American English in childhood.' *Studia Phonologica* 2: 27–39.

Neville, M. 1985. 'English language in Scottish schools.' Scottish Education Department report.

Newmark, L. 1981. 'Participatory observation: How to succeed in language learning' in H. Winitz (ed.) 1981.

Nunan, D. 1988. *Syllabus Design*. In the series: *Language Teaching: a Scheme for Teacher Education*. Oxford: Oxford University Press.

O'Neill, R. and **R. Scott.** 1974. *Viewpoints*. London: Longman.

Paris, S. and **B. Lindauer.** 1976. 'The role of inference in children's comprehension and memory for sentences.' *Cognitive Psychology* 8: 217–27.

Patterson, C. J. and **M. C. Kister.** 1981. 'The development of listener skills for referential communication' in W. P. Dickson (ed.): *Children's Oral Communication Skills.* New York: Academic Press.

Pica, T. and **C. Doughty.** 1985. 'The role of group work in classroom second language acquisition.' *Studies in Second Language Acquisition* 7/2: 233–48.

Pollack, I. and **J. Pickett.** 1963. 'The intelligibility of excerpts from conversation.' *Language and Speech* 6: 165–71.

Pratt, M. W., K. Bates, and **G. Wickers.** 1980. 'Checking it out: cognitive style and perceptual support as factors influencing message evaluation by young listeners and speakers.' Unpublished manuscript, Mount St Vincent University, Canada.

Rivers, W. M. 1971. 'Linguistic and psychological factors in speech perception and their implications for teaching materials' in P. Pimsleur and T. Quinn (eds.): *The Psychology of Second Language Learning.* Cambridge: Cambridge University Press.

Robinson, E. J. 1981. 'The child's understanding of inadequate messages and communication failure: a problem of ignorance or egocentrism?' in W. P. Dickson (ed.): *Children's Oral Communication Skills.* New York: Academic Press.

Robinson, E. J. and **W. P. Robinson.** 1977a. 'Children's explanations of communication failure and the inadequacy of the misunderstood message.' *Developmental Psychology,* 13: 156–61.

Robinson, E. J. and **W. P. Robinson.** 1977b. 'Development in the understanding of courses of success and failure in verbal communication.' *Cognition* 5: 363–78.

Schank, R. C. and **R. P. Abelson.** 1977. *Scripts, Plans, Goals and Understanding: an Enquiry into Human Knowledge Structure.* Hillsdale, NJ: Erlbaum.

Sharwood Smith, M. 1986. 'Comprehension versus acquisition: two ways of processing input.' *Applied Linguistics* 7/3: 239–56.

Shatz, M. 1978. 'Children's comprehension of question directives.' *Journal of Child Language* 5: 39–46.

Singer, J. and **J. Flavell.** 1981. 'Development of knowledge about communication: children's evaluation of explicitly ambiguous messages.' *Child Development* 52: 1211–15.

Small, M. and **J. Butterworth.** 1981. 'Semantic integration and the development of memory for logical inferences.' *Child Development* 52: 732–5.

Snow, C. 1977. 'The development of conversation between mothers and babies.' *Journal of Child Language* 4: 1–22.

Sonnenschein, S. 1982. 'The effects of redundant communication on listeners: when more is less.' *Child Development* 53: 717–29.

Sonnenschein, S. and **G. Whitehurst.** 1982. 'The effects of redundant communication on the behaviour of listeners: Does a picture need a thousand words?' *Journal of Psycholinguistic Research* 11/2: 115–25.

Steffenson, M. 1978. 'Satisfying inquisitive adults: some simple methods of answering yes/no questions.' *Journal of Child Language* 5: 221–36.

Stein, N. and **T. Nezworski.** 1978. 'The effects of organization and instructional set on story memory.' *Discourse Processes* 1:177–93.

Stokes, J. 1984. *Elementary Task Listening*. Cambridge: Cambridge University Press.

Swain, M. 1985. 'Communicative competence: some roles of comprehensible input and comprehensible output in its development' in S. Gass and C. Madden (eds.) 1985.

Tyler, L. 1983. 'The development of discourse mapping processes: the on-line interpretation of anaphoric expressions.' *Cognition* 13: 309–41.

Underwood, M. 1971. *Listen to This!* Oxford: Oxford University Press.

Underwood, M. 1976. *What a Story!* Oxford: Oxford University Press.

Underwood, M. 1979. *Have You Heard?* Oxford: Oxford University Press.

Underwood, M. and **P. Barr.** 1980. *Listeners.* (Series B: Work – 'Professions' and 'Unsocial Hours') Oxford: Oxford University Press.

Ur, P. 1984. *Teaching Listening Comprehension.* Cambridge: Cambridge University Press.

Voss, B. 1984. 'Perception of first language and second language texts—a comparative study.' *Bielefelder Beiträge zur Sprachlehrforschung* 13/2: 131–53.

Wallace, C. (forthcoming) *Reading.* In the series: *Language Teaching: a Scheme for Teacher Education.* Oxford: Oxford University Press.

Wallace, M. J. 1983. 'Survey of listening materials.' Appendix to Scottish Education Department *Interim Report: Listening Comprehension Project.* June 1983.

White, G. 1987. 'The Teaching of Listening Comprehension to Learners of English as a Foreign Language: a Survey.' M. Litt. dissertation, University of Edinburgh.

Widdowson, H. G. 1983. *Learning Purpose and Language Use.* Oxford: Oxford University Press.

Windeatt, S. 1981. 'A project in self-access learning for English language and study skills.' *Practical Papers in English Language Education.* Lancaster: University of Lancaster.

Winitz, H. (ed.) 1981. *The Comprehension Approach to Foreign Language Teaching.* Rowley, Mass.: Newbury House.

Wright, T. 1987. *Roles of Teachers and Learners.* In the series: *Language Teaching: a Scheme for Teacher Education.* Oxford: Oxford Unversity Press.

Yager, S., D. Johnson, and **R. Johnson.** 1985. 'Oral discussion, group to individual transfer and achievement in cooperative learning groups.' *Journal of Educational Psychology* 77: 60–6.

Appendices

Appendix 1 (for Tasks 79 and 99)

Cigarette consumption by adults in Scotland

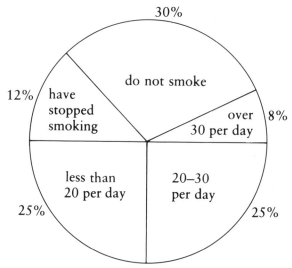

Diagram 2: *Speaker's version*

Guidelines for speaker
The intended problem points in the tapescript are given below in italics.

a circle with a line across the middle—students need to draw bottom half of the
   circle
outside them—it doesn't matter which is which, because they are both 25%
from the centre at an angle—to the right
the side of the circle—the right-hand side
to the other side—to the left
outside those—8% should go outside the small slice, 12% outside the medium
   slice, 30% outside the large one
in one of them—it doesn't matter which
in the other two—'do not smoke' goes in the 30% slice; 'over 30 per day' goes in
   the 8% slice

Appendix 2 (for Tasks 84 and 86)

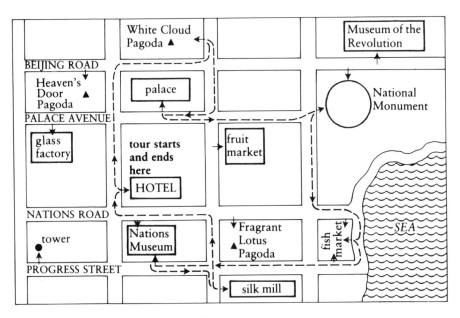

Map 1 (Tai Tu city tour): *Speaker's map*

Guidelines for speaker
The intended problem points in the tapescript are given below in italics.

we turn into the Beijing Road—turn right into Beijing Road
the White Cloud Pagoda—NB not Heaven's Door Pagoda
the National Monument—*statue* on Hearer's map
the market—the one the speaker means is the *fish market*
the Nations Museum—*museum* on Hearer's map. Between Progress Street and Nations Road
the silk mill—*factory* at the bottom of the Hearer's map

Index

Entries relate to Sections One, Two, and Three of the text, and to the glossary. References to the glossary are indicated by 'g' after the page number.